MICHIGAN'S
C. HAROLD WILLS

MICHIGAN'S
C. HAROLD WILLS

*The Genius Behind the Model T
and the Wills Sainte Claire Automobile*

ALAN NALDRETT AND LYNN LYON NALDRETT
FOR THE WILLS SAINTE CLAIRE MUSEUM

Foreword by Terry Ernest

THE
History
PRESS

Published by The History Press
Charleston, SC
www.historypress.net

All photos are from the collections of Terry Ernest, Alan Naldrett, the Wills Sainte Claire Museum and the Wills family.

First published 2017

Manufactured in the United States

ISBN 9781625859877

Library of Congress Control Number: 2017948454

Notice: The information in this book is true and complete to the best of our knowledge. It is offered without guarantee on the part of the authors or The History Press. The authors and The History Press disclaim all liability in connection with the use of this book.

CONTENTS

FOREWORD

I t is hard to consider where the automobile industry in the United States would be without the contributions of C. Harold Wills. As Henry Ford's first employee and chief engineer, Wills had a hand in every car Ford produced until Wills left in 1919, including the car that put the world on wheels, the Model T. His success at Ford propelled him to create his own car in the 1920s: the *Wills Sainte Claire*. Although Wills held many metallurgical patents, helped to create the world's most successful car, designed the famous Ford logo and built his own luxury car, there has never been a book written about this fascinating man.

Until now.

Alan Naldrett approached the board of directors of the Wills Sainte Claire Auto Museum and asked about the idea of writing a book about Wills. For many years, the board had been shopping for an author but had not had success in finding the right individual. To our great surprise, the right man had "fallen into our lap." Alan has done a great job putting all of the historical facts and anecdotes about Wills into book form.

Who was C. Harold Wills? To some, he was a wunderkind party boy who carried jewels in his pockets to impress his friends and "the ladies." To others, he was a mechanical genius who could solve complex problems associated with advances in the planetary transmission, complex steel blends and the large-scale production of vanadium and molybdenum steels. To another, smaller group, he was a husband, loving father and family man. From reading many articles (and reading between the lines) about him and studying him for more than thirty years, I can conclude that he was a man who was successful in nearly anything he put his mind to from an early age and never really experienced failure until his own car company filed for bankruptcy in the 1920s.

After Mr. Wills's endeavors at **Ford Motor Company**, he eventually made his way fifty miles north of Detroit to the small hamlet of Marysville. He purchased forty-four hundred acres of land to build his idea of the perfect automobile, in the process increasing the community's tiny population from two hundred to more than two thousand. He would lay out the town's streets, create neighborhoods by building houses, construct an industrial park and build the ideal community—it was known as the "community of contented living." A workman could purchase a house in Marysville on a lot "big enough for a vegetable garden" and escape the crowded living conditions of Detroit. Wills was not just building a new and fantastic automobile, he was also building a utopian community.

The car he built would not be any ordinary car. When he was at Ford, he learned how to build a simple and sturdy automobile. However, his dream was to build a fantastic car using the best technology and engineering concepts that the industry had ever seen.

The *Wills Sainte Claire* would be the first car to have a backup light and a patented courtesy light on the passenger side to illuminate the ground. It was one of the first cars to feature hydraulic brakes with an engine utilizing overhead cams.

A fantastic car, indeed.

Of the 12,107 cars made (according to Charles F. Boos, manager of the *Wills Sainte Claire* sales department), only about 80 remain today, making them quite rare.

I invite you to visit the Wills Sainte Claire Auto Museum in Marysville, Michigan, and see the largest collection of *Wills Sainte Claire* autos in the world.

I hope you enjoy learning about the history of C. Harold Wills and his endeavors as much as I have over the past thirty years!

Terry Ernest,
Director, Wills Sainte Claire Automobile Museum
Marysville, Michigan

ACKNOWLEDGEMENTS

We wish to thank Wills Sainte Claire Museum president and newsletter editor Terry Ernest and Wills Museum curator and secretary Carl Moss. The others on the Wills Sainte Claire Museum Board of Directors stepped up to help, including the following: Sally Wills Achatz, granddaughter of C. Harold Wills and fundraising manager for the museum; vice-president Pete Cangemi; merchandising director Paul Pawlosky; John Porter, in charge of the facilities; treasurer Scott Metzner; as well as many other longtime members, including Gary Wurmlinger, Bill Mason, Bill and Fran Minor, Vern Hansen and Ed Hausgen. Besides providing oral histories, they also helping to proofread, edit and check the manuscript for accuracy, with Terry and Carl doing the lion's share of the work.

Romie Minor of the National Automotive History Collection (NAHC) at the Detroit Public Library helped us obtain a lot of useful information, as did the Benson Ford Archive and the Wills Sainte Clair Museum archive. We also wish to thank History Press editors Katie Perry, Erin Owens, Krista Slavicek and Ben Gibson; Steven Rossi, who did proofing and fact-checking; as well as independent editors David Castle and Jessica Mehta. We wish we could include everybody, individually, who has recognized and helped preserve the genius, legacy and philanthropy of C.H. Wills.

INTRODUCTION

C. Harold Wills (June 1, 1878–December 30, 1940) was considered one of the greatest of the automobile pioneers by industry writers, auto enthusiasts and car collectors, as well as by the Automotive Hall of Fame. He was the designer of the world's top-selling car of all time, the car that put America on wheels, the *Model T*. Childe Harold Wills was not only the "right-hand man" of Henry Ford in his formative years but also the producer of the *Wills Sainte Claire*, considered by auto enthusiasts, mechanics and gearheads to be one of the finest cars ever manufactured.

Besides being a designer, Wills was a master metallurgist who pioneered the use of steel in cars. He improved vanadium steel, developing this lightweight material for use in the *Ford Model N, Model R, Model S* and *Model T.* He developed molybdenum steel for the mass-produced auto that carried his name.

Wills was also the master mechanic and engineer who developed the early planetary transmissions used in Ford's *Model T* and other autos. He developed tools and machinery used for assembly-line production.

When people consider the idea of a genius, they often refer to people who can think proficiently with both sides of their brain, such as Leonardo da Vinci, who was a great artist as well as a scientist. This "mark of genius" could easily apply to Wills. Besides his mechanical, engineering and scientific achievements, he used the "artistic" side in the creation of the Ford logo, which is still used today.

Wills considered himself a humanist. One example of this was his quest to make autos as comfortable as possible for both passengers and drivers. This was typified by the strategic placing of lights to make it easier for a passenger to find the curb and for the driver to change her flat tire. Wills also invented "back-up lights," making it easier for the driver to see what was behind him. Some said this innovation came about because of the many fire hydrants Wills had backed over. In that same regard, he invented the "brights" switch on headlights.

The other example of Wills's humanist side is his plan to build the "model worker's city" and provide for employees' basic needs, including housing, food and even recreation, the latter to alleviate the drudgery of assembly-line work. Maybe this was guilt on Wills's behalf, since he had helped develop the assembly-line system that accounted for much of the drudgery.

Wills hated his first name. The cause of much grief in his youth, the name, it is said, caused Wills to become an adept boxer. His mother, Mary, chose the name "Childe" because she liked the poet Lord Byron and got the name from Byron's *Childe Harold's Pilgrimage*. The name "Childe" was an honorific title used in thirteenth- and fourteenth-century England to denote a youth of noble birth awaiting knighthood.

Wills did everything he could to make people forget his first name. He referred to himself as C. Harold Wills, or simply C.H. Wills, his entire life. His first wife, Mabel, found out how much he detested the name when she had it printed on their wedding invitations. Wills insisted the whole batch of invitations be thrown out and new ones printed that didn't include "Childe."

Even on his tombstone in Woodlawn Cemetery in Detroit, which is next to the iconic Dodge brothers' mausoleum, there is only the initial "C." on Wills's marker, with no mention of "Childe."

C. Harold Wills went from being Henry Ford's trusted friend and accomplice on Ford's earliest cars to the chief engineer during the **Ford Motor Company**'s formative years and ultimately formed his own car company, building vastly superior and highly regarded autos. Wills was more than just an assistant to Ford; his ideas helped bring Ford's automotive ideas to fruition. Wills developed many of the earliest innovations of Ford's first models, including not only the transmission but also engine innovations such as removable, vertical cylinder heads. These innovations were first used in the **Ford Motor Company**'s earlier models and were successfully copied thereafter throughout Detroit's auto companies. Ford associate Ed "Spider" Huff said, "it was hard to know where Ford's work left off and Wills' began."

Henry Ford and C. Harold Wills, in a rare photo together.

Following his years at Ford, which left him a wealthy man, Wills still had many ideas he wanted to develop. After Henry Ford's success with the *Model T,* Ford felt it was the perfect car, one he could continue to produce and sell parts for forever. This spared Ford the cost of retooling factories and enabled him to control the parts market, which in the past had been farmed out to various manufacturers, such as the **Dodge Brothers**. The only changes Ford would allow to the *Model T* were electric lights in 1915, a painted radiator shell in 1916 and an optional self-starter in 1919 to replace the crank originally used to start the car manually.

Wills was not content to sit and collect royalty checks while his genius went to waste. He formed his own auto company and went on to produce many of the most praised autos in the industry.

1

THE EARLY YEARS OF
C. HAROLD WILLS

C. Harold Wills was the third, youngest and only surviving child of John Carnegie Wills (1835–1917) and Mary Swindell Wills (1836–1915). Sadly, an older brother and sister, Mary E. and John C. Jr., both died in 1875.

In 1832, Harold's grandfather John C. Wills emigrated from Forfar, Forfarshire, Scotland, to Canada, where Harold's father, John, was born in 1835. John Carnegie Wills moved to Fort Wayne, Indiana, driving a herd of sheep all the way! This is where Childe Harold Wills was born on June 1, 1878.

In 1880, the U.S. Census shows Wills and his parents at RR (Rural Route) 68, Allen County, Fort Wayne, Indiana. Wills's father's occupation is listed as "train dispatcher," and his mother's notation is "keeps house." It also mentions that she was born in Pennsylvania and her parents emigrated from England.

Wills lived in Fort Wayne until he was eight, when the family moved to 220 Twelfth Street in Detroit. His father was a railroad master mechanic and one of the first locomotive innovators. Harold picked up a love for mechanical engineering from him, as his father trained him in the use of machine tools.

Harold also had an affinity for commercial art, later indicated by his creation of the famed Ford logo. He often drew in his spare time when he was young and considered a career as a cartoonist or artist.

Will's father, John Carnegie Wills, taught young Wills about machine tools and mechanics.

In 1885, after the family moved to Detroit, Harold attended Detroit public schools and afterward furthered his education by reading trade journals. He took night courses in chemistry, metallurgy and mechanical engineering, although he probably learned as much from trial and error as he learned from textbooks. Later, he expressed his disdain for books to a newspaper interviewer: "If it's in a book, it's at least four years old and I don't have any use for it."

By all accounts, as a young man he had become tall, handsome and self-confident. He was described as having a dominant personality with strong persuasive abilities.

When the family moved to 1993 Trumbull Street in Detroit in 1895, seventeen-year-old Harold listed himself in the *Detroit City Directory* as an "artist boarding at home advertising for art jobs." With a paint set, he offered calligraphy services for business cards. The same year, he began a four-year apprenticeship to become a toolmaker at **Detroit Lubricator Company**, where his father worked as a manager. The company manufactured hydrostatic displacement lubricators.

Wills was offered $7.50 per week, which would go up to $10.00 once he was a full-fledged toolmaker. He knew this would always be a marketable trade. He took advantage of his toolmaking skills many times while at Ford, helping build the assembly-line system while designing, developing and organizing the tools and huge machinery used to build automobiles. However, at his original apprenticeship, after the four years were up, he had only been given one pay increase. Since he wasn't paid the increases he was promised, he started job hunting.

His next job was in a toolmaking shop where his skills were recognized and appreciated. Wills's starting salary was eighteen dollars per week, a princely increase from his former paycheck. On top of that, in just three weeks he moved up the ranks to become chief engineer and foreman at twenty-seven dollars a week. His hard work, long hours and perseverance were further rewarded when, after three months, he became the plant superintendent at fifty dollars a week. In only six months, he had increased

Wills is seen here in his twenties. Despite working on car engines and being covered in grease and grime, he always looked well dressed.

his pay from ten dollars per week to fifty dollars, a 400 percent increase. With all his promotions, he moved out of his parents' house in 1904 and into Detroit's Plaza Hotel.

In the early 1900s, it was very popular to take up residence in a hotel. The Plaza was near the site of the Detroit Athletic Club, where Wills became a member. (The Coldwell clock he donated to them is still displayed near the second-floor elevators at the club.) Not far away from the Plaza was the Russell House on Congress Street near the Campus Martius, the gathering place for Detroit's movers and shakers until 1907.

Even though he was gainfully employed and making good money, Wills was young and restless. He answered an ad originated by the man who would have the greatest impact on his life: Henry Ford. After meeting, the two men discovered a mutual love for mechanics, engineering and tinkering with motors. They also shared an interest in leisure activities, including hunting, fishing and boating.

Thanks to their mutual fascination for machines, Wills was soon using his drawing and drafting skills to flesh out Ford's automotive visions, which Ford often sketched on the back of an envelope or napkin. Even though Ford had studied mechanical drawing at the **Detroit Business Institute**, he was not proficient at reading a blueprint, much less drawing one. Ford's method was called "cut and try." He hadn't developed a blueprint until Wills came along. Wills began using both his drawing and mechanical skills to interpret and improve Ford's ideas.

Wills had a unique ability to detect flaws in a drawing design and correct it on the drawing board before putting it into production. The fact that he could explain his reasoning to Ford assured his immediate future. As soon as Wills joined with Ford, Ford's engineering work took a swing upward, as Wills became the one-man engineering department.

Before Henry Ford met Wills, he was known around Detroit as a mechanical type and a bicycle enthusiast. He tinkered in a coal shed at the back of his rented house on Bagley Street in Detroit where he built his first vehicle, the Quadricycle. However, once complete, it wouldn't fit through the door of the shed. He hadn't thought to measure the space needed to get the vehicle out. Ford solved the problem by grabbing an axe and chopping at the wood and brick around the door until the opening was large enough to accommodate the vehicle. Unfortunately, he only rented the property. The landlord later permitted a larger door to be installed.

When Henry Ford built the Quadricycle in 1896, he became the second person to drive his car down Woodward Avenue, the main street of Detroit. The first automobile was driven on Woodward on March 6, 1896, when Charles King and his assistant, Oliver Barthel, drove down the avenue. On their first ride, Henry Ford followed them on his bicycle. King and Barthel were among Ford's early cohorts in the construction of an automobile.

Ford was working at Thomas Edison's **Edison Illuminating Company** when he showed the great inventor his motor vehicle powered by a gasoline engine. Edison told him he was "headed in the right direction," even though it was well known that Edison had expressed a preference for electric autos. (Edison had tried marketing his own electric car and had even designed a popular battery for use in cars, one that allowed the vehicle to travel 211 miles before recharging.) This praise from Ford's hero encouraged him to build a second car, secure funding and start his first car company.

The **Detroit Automobile Company** was formed on August 5, 1899. The *Detroit City Directory* of 1900 lists C. Harold Wills as a draftsman for the company and Henry Ford as the superintendent. Wills was also an officer of the board, as Ford wanted to keep Wills around enough to award him an important position in his first company. The company was headquartered at 1343 Cass Avenue in Detroit.

Ford felt the cars produced by his first company were of too low a quality to be marketed. There were problems with the ignition and carburetor. The car would only run for minutes at a time before shutting down. Not admitting defeat, Ford had his workers continue to make parts that wouldn't be used. The investors were not happy, so they and Ford dissolved the company in January 1901.

Wills felt he wasn't advancing fast enough and left Ford's employ to work as an engineer at the **Boyer Machine Company**, which became the **Burroughs Adding Machine Company** in 1905.

2

WORKING WITH HENRY FORD

W ills advanced as quickly in his new job at Boyer as he had at the toolmaking shop, and within a year he was the chief engineer and assistant to the president of the company. However, at this point in his life, with so many options available to him, he was restless. He began to think that he had already "reached the top as a toolmaker" and could not rise any higher at **Boyer Machine Company**.

This was his mood when, one night on a street corner as he waited for the streetcar, he struck up a conversation with an older, successful businessman.

The man told him, "Success is not difficult. All of us have opportunities. But the trouble is that too often we are not prepared for them when they come." In his later years, Wills cited this remark as the reason he got back in touch with Henry Ford after they had first worked together.

While working at the **Boyer Machine Company**, Wills had become reacquainted with Ford and reassessed his future. He decided he wanted to be involved with Ford's motor vehicle endeavors and proposed a deal only a workaholic would consider. Wills would not quit his job, but he would work for Ford from 5:00 a.m. to 7:00 a.m., then go to work at Boyer. In the evening, he would return to Ford's workspace and work from 7:00 p.m. until midnight.

Henry Ford wasn't terribly young—he was thirty-four when he began working with the twenty-one-year-old Wills in 1899 and 1900. Ford longed to turn his automotive obsession into a profession, and Wills realized that. This caused Wills to think that maybe this was his big opportunity, after all.

Wills would regularly meet Ford at 81 Park Place in downtown Detroit, where Ford had rented a workspace from Barton Peck in the back of Peck's bicycle repair shop. Since the workshop didn't have heat (they couldn't afford coal for the stove), during the cold Detroit winter Ford and Wills would don boxing gloves and spar for a while until the circulation in their hands returned. This warmed their hands enough for them to resume working on their projects.

Barton Peck was the son of another well-known citizen of Detroit, Josiah Peck, and one of Ford's early friends in the 1890s, when they were both bicycle devotees. During the Gay Nineties, the nation was enthralled by bicycles and bicycling. This included Barton Peck, owner of the bicycle shop, and Henry Ford. Many of the roads later used by early motorcars existed due to bicycle enthusiasts calling for better streets to ride on.

The next step beyond bicycles was developing motorized vehicles. The small space in the back of Peck's bike shop was where a lot of early Detroit motorcar experimentation took place. Barton Peck would, with the help of King, Barthel and Ford, become the third person to drive a car of their own construction on the streets of Detroit.

Wills became one of the people closest to Ford for many years, accompanying him on fact-finding trips, car races and even visits to taverns. When the Pontchartrain Hotel was built, the hotel bar became the main gathering place for the automakers of Detroit. John and Horace Dodge, William Durant, Harold Wills, Henry Leland, Louis Chevrolet, Henry Ford and scores of others would brainstorm into the night. The next morning, the bar would be littered with sketches and blueprints of car transmissions, crankshafts and motors. Henry Ford attended these gatherings only to soak up the ideas and ambience—he wouldn't drink alcohol. (Interestingly, Leland was at first a hard drinker, but in 1915, he found religion and wrote a tract against "demon rum.")

Ford, with Wills's expertise, was ready to start another company in 1902. The **Henry Ford Company** was funded by many of the same personages who had provided financing for the **Detroit Automobile Company**. Wills was once again a draftsman for one of Ford's companies. On August 4, 1902, Wills received his first written contract to work for the **Henry Ford Company**, becoming the firm's first official employee.

Funded by coal tycoon Alexander Malcomson, Ford and Wills split $125 per month. Ford had known Malcomson for years; Malcomson had delivered coal to the Ford family farm. As coal was a needed fuel in those days, Malcomson became rich—his coal company was the largest in the

The Ford factory at 697 Mack Avenue in Detroit was a converted barn. After its stint as a Ford factory, it started manufacturing Cadillacs, under the leadership of Henry Leland.

state. Its motto was "Hotter than Sunshine." If nothing else, Ford could at least get enough coal to heat their workshop!

In December 1902, Ford and Wills unveiled a "sample commercial vehicle" designed for Malcomson.

Wills and Ford came up with a new idea for their car engines. They set the two cylinders of the car vertically instead of horizontally. This reduced engine wear and vibration and thereby increased power. This reduced the use of the flywheel.

Ford and the stockholders did not get along, especially since progress was slow on building cars. Ford was not happy and quit—or he was asked to leave, depending on the account one reads. Wills left with Ford.

A local engine builder, Henry Leland, was called to appraise the factory and its contents in anticipation of liquidation. Leland had his own auto design and convinced the stockholders to keep the factory open while they market his auto. This firm went on to become the **Cadillac Motor Company**. (Henry Ford would even the score with Leland for taking over his company years later, after Leland had formed the **Lincoln Motor Company**. When Leland's new company foundered, Henry Ford bought it at a bargain price, $8.8 million.)

After leaving his second company, Ford obtained funding from a champion bicycle rider, Tom Cooper, who wanted to branch out into auto racing. He hired Ford and Wills to build him a race car.

Thomas "Tommy" Cooper was a bicycle-racing superstar in the Gay Nineties, when bicycles were the fad of the land and bicycle racing was one of the most popular sports. He won the Bicycle Championship of America from 1896 through 1899, as well as numerous other races. Cooper became quite wealthy from the winnings.

Since Tom Cooper was one of his heroes, Henry Ford was elated when the racer commissioned him to put together a car for him. With Wills doing most of the work, two race cars were assembled. The one that was to be Cooper's was the Red Devil, and the one Ford intended to keep was the 999. The 999 was named for the *Empire State Express,* a New York Central locomotive that made a record-breaking run between Chicago and New York, setting a speed record of more than 112 miles per hour.

The 999's first race was the Manufacturers' Challenge Cup in Grosse Pointe, Michigan, on October 25, 1902. Wills was on the race crew. Both Cooper and Ford were afraid that the car was too unpredictable for either of them to drive—it could generate eighty horsepower! Cooper introduced Ford to Barney Oldfield, a bicycle racer he knew. Oldfield agreed to drive the 999, the car with a four-cylinder engine and a two-handed tiller for steering. A four-cylinder engine was twice the power of the usual two- and one-cylinder cars available in 1902.

Oldfield, who had never driven a race car before, spent a week learning how to drive the car. He went on to win the race. He also set a new land speed record of one mile in a little more than a minute. It was the beginning of a successful career transition from bicycle racer to race-car driver for Oldfield.

After this adventure, Ford and Cooper parted ways. Henry's wife, Clara, was glad, because, she said, "He thinks too much of low-down women to suit me." She probably said "I told you so" when Cooper lost his life as one of the first drunk-driving fatalities. On November 12, 1906, he was killed racing in New York's Central Park in the early-morning hours. He was in his *Matheson* automobile when, after midnight, he was challenged and raced—straight into a stalled car. Cooper clipped the car, causing him to swerve sharply. The accident occurring in the days before seat belts, all of the passengers were tossed out.

His two female passengers were taken to the hospital, one in critical condition. Tom was killed instantly, his chest crushed and his head mangled

The race car 999 was famous for breaking the world's land speed record and the place it had in the success of the **Ford Motor Company**. It set a world record on January 9 and then did it again for an "official" timer on January 12, 1904.

by the steering wheel. Passenger Daniel Barlow died of his injuries a few hours later in the hospital. Cooper was taken back to Detroit to be buried in the family plot in Woodmere Cemetery.

By the time of the car's second race on January 9, 1904, Ford felt he was ready to drive it himself—as long as it wasn't held on a circular track, which Ford disliked. The auto was loaded on to the Detroit United Railway Interurban Train and taken to the New Baltimore stop, where it was unloaded and taken down New Baltimore's Washington Street to Anchor Bay. The race car had a wooden chassis but no hood or body, so transporting it less than a mile from the stop to the bay was not very difficult.

The race "crew" included Harold Wills, Ford's wife, Clara, his ten-year-old son Edsel, John Wandersee and Ed "Spider" Huff. This was Ford's main entourage in the early days.

The crew stayed at the hotel on the blistery cold weekend. Two different runs with the 999 race car were made in attempts to break the world speed record. John Dodge, James Couzens and Alexander Malcomson were also present that weekend to view the races.

Every entourage has a "strange" member, and Spider Huff was this one's. Ford hated Spider's tobacco chewing, but the mechanic, electrician and engineer was otherwise valuable and a friend to Ford. (With Spider riding in the car with Ford during the race, Ford had installed a spittoon in the race car.) Ford even tolerated Spider treating his depression by disappearing into bars and houses of ill repute for days at a time.

Wills had introduced Ford to John F. Wandersee, who had started as a sweeper in Ford's first plant. Wills and Ford arranged to have Wandersee educated in the fields of chemistry and metallurgy by sending him to study vanadium steel at United Steel Alloy (later the United Steel Company) in Canton, Ohio. Wandersee worked with Wills to advance knowledge in the field.

Wills spent most of his time in New Baltimore tinkering with the 999 (by Ford's account, the Red Devil) in the cold, at a shack in the back of their hotel. Harold was familiar with working in the cold, having toiled with Ford at the 81 Park Place workshop.

The entourage stayed at the Hotel Chesterfield, a large, three-story hotel not far from the waterfront of Anchor Bay, which was an inlet of Lake St. Clair. The hotel was known for its amenities, including electric lights and steam heat. It appealed to a clientele that would be likely to buy a Ford car. It was hoped that, in addition to the publicity for the car, they might attract a few more financiers.

The hotel sponsored the event and advertised it as automobile racing, but a smaller line of text on the flyer betrayed its true purpose: "Henry Ford of the **Ford Motor Works** of Detroit will attempt to lower the World Record." More copy on the flyer allowed that, starting at 2:00 p.m., Ford would make as many attempts as needed to, in his words, "make a mile in 36 seconds." (The poster further stated that there would also be an iceboat race for a "valuable prize.")

A four-mile raceway was cleared on the frozen lake and covered with cinders. It was a straight track, as Ford had requested. Wills gave the engine a last check before Ford started. The track looked smooth but was actually quite rough. Ford would hit a rift in the difficult-to-navigate ice and, suddenly, would be airborne! This happened a few times. On some occasions, the vehicle landed on its side. Ford thought the car was airborne more than it was on the ground. According to local lore, Ford never paid the five dollars he promised to a local man for clearing the ice and spreading cinders, perhaps in retaliation for the roughness of the track.

Finally, on January 9, Wills tinkered with the engine some more, and Ford managed to get the vehicle going fast enough to set a new world land-speed record of 91.37 miles per hour. He had achieved his goal of going a mile in thirty-six seconds! However, Ford's racing career almost came to a quick end when he nearly collided with a wooden schooner trapped in the ice.

The Hotel Chesterfield, where the Ford entourage stayed in their quest to break the world speed record. Henry Ford liked the muskrat dinner served here. The Hotel Chesterfield was the sponsor of the event.

Afterward, the Ford entourage stayed at the Hotel Chesterfield. The hotel treated them to a roast muskrat feast, which Ford pronounced "delicious!" The dinner recipients included Wills, Wandersee, Huff and Clara and Edsel Ford.

Ford's own account of the race contradicts this story. He said that he and his driving assistant (Spider) were so elated that they built a fire and cooked a muskrat right there on the ice. All other accounts, including his wife's, state that the hotel treated them to the meal. Perhaps Ford so relished the roast muskrat served to him by the hotel that he had the food wrapped up in a doggie bag that he took out on the ice with him and reheated.

An incident in the lobby of the Chesterfield Hotel was related in an article in the 1937 *Gasoline Age*, on page 66. While at the hotel, a few days later, on January 12, 1904, Ford and Wills tinkered with a nickel slot machine in the lobby. After fooling around with the machinery, the two men were amused as Paul Bruske, a newspaper reporter, proceeded to lose all his nickels in the machine. Bruske was initially insulted as Wills quizzed him about how many nickels he had lost in the machine, telling Wills it was none of his business.

Finally, he consented to tell Wills how much he had lost if Wills would tell him why he was so interested. Wills explained that he and Henry Ford had seen the slot machine in the Hotel Chesterfield's lobby while they

Henry Ford in forefront on ice of Anchor Bay in January 1904, while on the ice to set a new world speed record. Wills, sitting, is marked with an arrow.

were resting by the stove. They speculated about how the coins came out, in quantities determined accurately "according to the figure in which the speculative nickel had been inserted, and the figure at which the whirling multi-colored wheel stopped." They studied the machine through the opaque walls. As time went on, they dropped nickels to test their theory and the mental blueprint they had made of the machine.

They eventually determined that a wire inserted in one of the nickel slots would find a lever. Moving this lever, they could manipulate it to release all the nickels contained within the machine, which it did. It is illustrative of Wills's good character that he felt obliged to return to Bruske all the money he had lost.

Another run with the race car was attempted after the one on January 9. On January 12, the speed record was attempted again, with similar results. Since nobody from the American Automobile Association had been there on January 9 to time the run, it wasn't considered "official." Thus, Ford repeated it on January 12 with similar results, with the AAA official in attendance. The run on the ice on January 12 became an official record.

Accounts of the Ford world record on Anchor Bay differ. Most accounts don't mention that he set the record on January 9 and repeated it on January 12, 1904. Also, some accounts say Ford was in the 999, while Ford's own report states that he was in the Arrow (also known as the Red Devil). (The most detailed account is given by Henry's wife, Clara, in the Ford R. Bryan biography about her.) What is definite is that the record lasted only about twenty days, even though Ford had beat the old one by better than six seconds. On January 27, 1904, Ford was in the audience in Ormond Beach, Florida, when William Vanderbilt, son of Commodore Vanderbilt, upped the record to 92.3 miles per hour from Ford's 91.37. Vanderbilt drove a four-cylinder *Mercedes*.

Ford developed the 999 to win races and gain a good reputation for the cars he produced. He again recruited Wills to help with the design. Wills again spent all the off-hours from his regular job working with Ford in their rented workshop, building Ford's famous race cars, the 999 and the Arrow.

Both cars were nearly identical, and both looked like stripped-down models of the cars of the day. The Arrow was painted red to distinguish it from the 999, and it was sometimes called the Red Devil. The 999 is considered by many to be the first car built for racing, and Wills is considered its chief architect. Ford once uncharacteristically confessed that Wills was "the man the public think I am."

With his newfound racing fame, Ford again courted coal baron Alexander Malcomson to help finance his next car company. On June 16, 1903, Ford's third venture, the **Ford Motor Company**, was incorporated. Ford pledged to give 25 percent of the first 30 percent of his stock dividends to Wills, since Wills didn't have enough money to invest in company stock. When the Ford dividend amount became $1 million per year, it was capped at that amount. Wills was generous, giving part of his dividend checks to his closest associates.

There were many accounts of Wills's generosity, as well as stories of another side of Wills. "In order to get along with Mr. Ford, you had to have a little mean streak in your system," said a Ford associate, Max Wollering. "You had to be tough and mean. Mr. Ford enjoyed that." Wollering also remarked how Wills and Ford seemed to not trust each other and would watch each other all the time. Regardless, it was obvious, especially in the early days, how much Ford felt he needed Wills and his expertise.

Wills in his early years was described as a taskmaster, insisting that his staff drive themselves as much as he drove himself. This was a quality Henry Ford liked. Ford didn't like job titles. He wanted his employees to work on whatever task he needed them to perform at the time, regardless of job title. Although Wills was originally described as "chief engineer" or "manufacturing manager" of **Ford Motor Company**, during most of his tenure at Ford he was mainly known by others as "Ford's right-hand man."

Ford was later known to assume credit for many accomplishments of his staff, such as Wills's work on vanadium steel. Early on, though, Ford had no problem with the company newsletter, *Ford Times,* describing Wills as directing "the entire working of the manufacturing department."

3

"CHIEF ENGINEER" OF FORD MOTOR COMPANY

From 1903 to 1912, Wills was the chief designer and engineer on every car that Ford manufactured, the pinnacle being the *Model T*. Besides serving as engineer and designer, Wills was also the metallurgist for the company. "Chief Engineer" and "Chief Designer" were unofficial titles however. Ford did not like giving his top brass titles so that he could be free to move them around at will.

By the end of 1903, the company had outgrown the rented former wagon factory on Mack Avenue and acquired land to start building what would become known as the Piquette Plant. By early 1905, the factory was completed and the Ford operations moved in. It was located on Piquette Avenue at Beaubien Street. This was in the "Milwaukee Junction" section of Detroit, popular with the growing number of Detroit automakers. Largely because of the area's proximity to two different railroad lines, it was at one time essential for shipping in raw materials and shipping out completed automobiles. Auto companies headquartered in Milwaukee Junction, besides the early **Ford Motor Company**, included early stalwarts **Studebaker**, **EMF**, **Hupp** and **Packard Motor Companies**, as well as **Paige**, **Northern** and **Wayne**. The proximity of these companies helped new technology spread among them, a trait attributed to Detroit's beating out Cleveland, Ohio, and Indianapolis, Indiana, to become the undisputed "Motor City."

The Piquette Plant had ten times the space as the Mack Avenue factory. Wills's office was located on the second floor, behind the corner office of

Henry Ford. The cars were built on the third floor, and an elevator was used to lower the cars to the ground floor. The press was informed that the company was now employing more than three hundred men.

Wills and Ford worked together on the Ford *Models A, B, C, F, N, S, R* and *T*. Business was good, as each model was a step up from the last. Around Christmas 1902, with some assistance from John and Horace Dodge, Wills had a prototype *Model A* completed. But they thought they could do better and started at once to build a second prototype. This was especially fortunate, since Wills had one of Detroit's first major auto accidents when he totaled the first prototype while driving with mechanic Gus Degener down Mack Avenue. Luckily, they weren't seriously injured, and fortunately, they had mostly completed the second prototype. The remains of the first prototype were stored under the staircase of the Piquette Plant. The accident might have made Wills more safety-conscious, because he later developed the first back-up lights for cars, as well as other safety equipment.

Most of the *Model A*'s parts were manufactured elsewhere and assembled in the Mack Avenue factory. In 1905, Ford formed the **Ford Manufacturing Company**, separate from the main company, to manufacture auto parts. Wills was the secretary and a stockholder.

Besides being an expert mechanic and draftsman, Wills was a metallurgist. He developed many alloys that allowed lightweight, durable auto parts to be built. Wills developed a four-cylinder engine block with a detachable cylinder head and a transverse leaf-spring suspension that was used on all the early Fords.

One of the most well-known contributions Wills made was the "planetary transmission" used in the *Model T* and other Fords. The *Model T* was a rear-wheel drive vehicle with what was called a "three-speed" transmission. Today, this would be called a "two-speed" transmission, since one of Ford's three speeds was reverse. The transmission was controlled by three foot pedals and a lever next to the driver's seat.

The "planetary" aspect of the transmission was so named because a gear, the "planet" gear, revolved around the "sun" gear while rotating on its axis. A lever on the steering wheel was the throttle. Wills said he came up with the concept while soaking in the bathtub. In fact, as he told his son C. Harold Wills Jr., he would soak in the bathtub in the morning, and it was there that he did his best thinking and got his best ideas.

Besides his mechanical contributions, Wills also helped develop the assembly-line system used at Ford. The system was first developed as an experiment, starting in July 1908, on Sundays at the Piquette Plant. Charlie

Lewis, an assembly foreman, would pull a chassis along a rope, while Wills and others would add parts to it along the way, until a vehicle was completed. Wills and the others studied other innovations of the day, such as conveyor belts used at canning factories.

The Ford assembly line had several differences from the assembly line at the Olds factory, which was initiated a few years earlier. One innovation came after Ford made a trip to the meat market before going to work. He noticed the meat hooks, which gave him an idea on how to move a chassis along the assembly line.

Ford asked Wills to negotiate contracts on his behalf. Since Wills had a gift for tool and machinery design, he handled a lot of the machinery purchases. He became the one to deal directly with **Hyatt Roller Bearing**, a Ford supplier since 1904. Wills dealt with its sales manager, Alfred Sloan, who later became head of **General Motors**. Wills derived price concessions from Sloan because of Ford's volume buying. Alfred Sloan leaned about vanadium steel from Wills and took the knowledge with him to **General Motors**. Sloan later famously remarked that Wills was an "innovative genius."

Wills also brought many knowledgeable people to Ford, helping it grow into a powerhouse auto company. This included the chief innovator and general superintendent at Ford, the company's fifth employee, Peter "Ed" Martin. Wills also introduced master engineer Joseph Galamb, who initially served as Wills's assistant. Galamb would also be credited by Wills as a co-designer of the *Model T*.

Vanadium consists of nickel and chrome added to steel. Wills often experimented with nickel and manganese. Vanadium's use in the *Model T*'s chassis is one of the reasons for its success—vanadium's tensile strength was almost three times that of regular steel, yet it was easier to manipulate and more lightweight.

Ford and Wills first became aware of vanadium at a Palm Beach, Florida race in 1905. A French race car exploded, and Ford picked up a piece, a small valve strip stem, and showed it to Wills. Wills was amazed at the lightness and strength of the metal and realized it was smelted differently than the American way. The method originated in England. Wills went on to study vanadium. He hired a firm in Canton, Ohio, to use a small part of its plant to produce the first lightweight but strong, nickel-chrome vanadium steel produced on the North American continent.

In 1907, Ford began introducing the metal on *Models N*, R and S before using it extensively on the *Model T*. It was one of the reasons the *Model T* was so popular. Wills would eventually be instrumental in developing and using molybdenum, an even stronger steel, in the *Wills Sainte Claire* auto.

Wills was a pioneer in the notion that cars did not need to weigh a lot. This thought was behind his quest for durable yet lightweight sources of metal. Wills felt that great weight placed restrictions on the speed and pick-up of a vehicle.

Wills's artistic talent was used not only to render faultless blueprints. In 1906, he created the iconic Ford logo that has been used, with only slight variations, on every Ford auto. Wills knew that the fledgling company needed a permanent logo. (There had been complaints about the lackluster original one.) He rummaged around his attic until he came across the painting set from his youth. He had used it to make extra cash by printing "visiting cards." (In a custom of the day, people left calling cards if the person they came to visit was not home.) With the painting set, Wills created the flowing script of the Ford logo, which has been used in many variations ever since. The script was meant to mimic Henry Ford's signature.

4

SUCCESS AND RICHES

As the **Ford Motor Company** became more successful, Wills moved out of the Palace Hotel in 1904 and into a house at 39 Bethune Avenue in Detroit. He married Mabel Preston (October 1, 1874–August 27, 1942) on June 16, 1904, with Henry Ford as the best man, not long after the **Ford Motor Company** became successful. The couple then moved to 1760 East Jefferson Avenue in Detroit.

Wills's large, opulent, waterfront house on Jefferson included a dock for his yacht and other boats. The boathouse protected many of Wills's powerboats and other watercraft but was not large enough for his yacht. The house had a cupola where Wills and his family would often sit and enjoy the view. (At one time, Wills had paid famed architect Frank Lloyd Wright to design a house for him, but it was never built.)

As Wills's wealth continued to grow, he had more fun. When he received his first $1,000 bonus, he converted it into $1 bills and threw them in the air at his home, delighting his wife and daughters. In later years, Wills had a huge toboggan slide erected at his Jefferson Avenue house.

Wills served as a bridge between Ford and the other, typically imbibing, auto pioneers. Wills was not a teetotaler like Ford—the $4,000-plus monthly wine bills for the Wills house reflect this. Wills followed the example of many of the auto barons who worked hard and played harder, such as Billy Durant, Walter Flanders, Carl Fisher (who died of alcoholism), the Chevrolet brothers and the Dodge brothers. Roy D. Chapin, one of the Hudson Motor Company's founders, was one of the leaders in the fight

Mabel Preston Wills married C. Harold Wills in 1904. Henry Ford was the best man.

Mabel Wills in the garden.

to repeal Prohibition. However, Wills could relate to the teetotaling Ford and still work with the Dodge brothers, probably the most well known of the hard-partying barons. They were known for their propensity to destroy small "workingmen's bars" at night and show up the next day to pay for the damages (if they remembered where it was). One exception to their usual, low-priced taverns was when they were celebrating their first auto (co-designed by Wills) at the elegant ballroom of the Book-Cadillac Hotel in Detroit. The climax of the evening was when John Dodge stood on a table and used his cane to smash out all the bulbs in the Tiffany chandeliers. The party ended as the entire ballroom went dark. And some people said he was the quiet one!

The Dodge brothers would often hire two-fisted drinkers like themselves. Sometimes, they would have to go into local bars and drag their men back to work. This led to the Dodge factory allowing kegs of beer and drinking within the facility, to keep the men from wandering off the assembly line.

Henry Ford would often boast about how much he learned from being a nondrinker while others were imbibing. In later years, many of the denizens of the Pontchartrain bar days expressed a certain resentment that Ford was "not one of the guys" and may have been somehow taking advantage of everyone else by staying sober. Truly, Ford's lighter moments were always said to involve practical jokes done at the expense of others. For example,

Wills off for a ride in an early Ford car he designed.

Wills and his wife, Mabel, in another Wills-designed Ford car.

Ford whittled wooden croutons and put them in Harvey Firestone's soup, then laughed joyously as the hapless Harvey tried to bite into them.

Wills enjoyed hunting and fishing and contributed to conservation causes. He also played tennis and was a member of the Detroit Racquet Club. He was said to be dapper, always well dressed and a "ladies' man."

Wills belonged to the Anchor Club, the Bloomfield Hills Country Club, the Detroit Boat Club and the Detroit Yacht Club. He also belonged to the Detroit Country Club, the Detroit Club, the Oakland Hills Country Club, the Detroit Polo Club, the Detroit Golf Club, the American Society of Mechanical Engineers, the Old Club and the Detroit Aviation Club.

Wills's yacht was named *Marold* (a combination of Mabel and Harold Wills's first names). It was convenient that Wills's second wife was named Mary—he didn't have to change the name of his yacht. He also owned several smaller speedboats. *Baby Marold* was the name of a step hydroplane that brothers Jack and Martin Beebe, renowned boat makers from Marine City, Michigan, designed for him. Marine City is just downriver from Marysville. Jack Beebe was later the head of engineering at Wills's Marysville auto factory.

Wills's powerboat *Baby Marold* competed for the Gold Cup of the American Power Boat Association (APBA) hydroplane race, held in Detroit in 1916.

The boat was in the lead when it caught fire. It was sunk by the Coast Guard to prevent further damage to it. It was then towed back to Wills's Detroit boathouse. Despite the mishap, Wills maintained his interest in the sport and was on the board of the APBA for years.

Besides boat racing, tennis, duck hunting and fishing, Wills loved jewels and was known to carry them in his pocket. He would wear them in stickpins, cufflinks and rings. When he was single, he would pull them out of his pocket to dazzle prospective dates. He would later give jewels to his wives and even his friends.

In 1906, Mabel and Harold's first child, a son, lived only an hour. They then had two daughters, Virginia (November 22, 1908–April 16, 1997) and Josephine (April 26, 1910–May 15, 1914). The couple divorced in 1913 after six years of marriage.

Uncharacteristically, Wills's children from both marriages and both of his wives are buried in the same large area of Woodlawn Cemetery in Detroit, where Wills had purchased two large lots. The plots are next to the Dodge brothers' mausoleum.

By 1912, with the **Ford Motor Company** moved into the Highland Park plant, Wills was said to be at the height of his influence. He had his pick of secretaries from the company secretarial pool and chose Evangeline Cote, a vivacious, nineteen-year-old French Canadian. She had been with the

While still at Ford Motor Company, Wills became interested in boat racing. The *Baby Marold* was a speedboat of Wills, which he used in racing competitions. He is at the wheel in this photo.

Wills's friends and family gather for a photo on the dock, following another race with Wills's boat the *Baby Marold*.

company for three years and had risen to become head of the stenographic department. She was just over five feet tall, with bright eyes, and Wills at first took a shine to her, offering her the jewels he often carried around with him and showed off at the slightest provocation. (He also liked jewels for their investment value.)

But Wills wasn't the only one showing an interest in Ms. Cote. Wills and Ford would meet many times in 1914 and 1915 as they discussed improving the moving assembly line and implementing the daily wage of five dollars. (Wills was in favor of the higher wage, contrary to what Couzens and other Ford stalwarts thought.) As such, Ford had many opportunities to become acquainted with Evangeline Cote.

Cote moved from being Wills's secretary to working directly for Ford. In 1944, one of her first projects was arranging for the move of Henry Ford's birthplace farmhouse to Greenfield Village. As time went on, she was often rumored to be Ford's mistress. Cote married Ford's main mechanic, Joe Dahlinger, and they had an estate next to Ford's Fair Lane Estate in Dearborn.

Although close friends in their early days, Ford and Wills grew further apart as the years wore on. Wills was critical of Ford and his ideas and felt that he had the superior intellect. Although he was called a perfectionist, Wills was described as pleasant and easy to work with.

However, Ford and Wills were still close enough as late as 1916 for Ford to ask Wills to accompany him to a meeting with the Dodge brothers, who were complaining about **Ford Motor Company** resources being used for Ford's separate endeavor, **Fordson**. Henry was using this company, of "Ford and Son," to develop tractors and other farm equipment.

Over time, Henry Ford became much different than the affable, kind gentleman he had been before the success of the *Model T*. After the success of that car, Ford began to change. In his youth, he would associate mostly with mechanics and designers. After the *Model T*'s phenomenal success, his friends tended to be people like famed inventor Thomas Edison and tire tycoon Harvey Firestone, superstars of their day, just as Ford had become.

As he became more successful, Ford also became more autocratic and began to exert control over his employees in less-than-subtle ways. He had a separate department dedicated to policing the morals of the workers and their families. Wills's future partner, John Lee, was the head of Ford's sociological department. Lee also led **Ford Motor Company**'s profit-sharing department.

Formed by Lee and Henry Ford in 1914, the sociological department created a set of rules for employees to follow in order to receive their five-dollar daily wage from **Ford Motor Company**. These rules of conduct included stipulations regarding each employee's alcohol consumption, cleanliness and spending habits.

The sociological department hired agents who would pop in to employees' houses unannounced and check that the rules were being followed. They would also monitor employee banking records and their children's school attendance records. Men who were more than twenty-two years old had to be married or they could no longer be employed by Ford.

On the other hand, the controversial department also provided free English lessons for immigrants. Immigrants were guided toward attaining U.S. citizenship, and national patriotism was required. The company provided doctors and legal assistance as needed, as well as cheap financing for home purchases. **Ford Motor Company** also provided one of the safest working environments of the time, although this wasn't saying a lot. In the early 1900s, factory work was still hard and hazardous, no matter where workers were employed.

5

BUILDING HENRY FORD'S PERFECT CAR

Wills was the primary designer of all models of the early **Ford Motor Company**. The second 1903 *Model A* prototype that Ford and Wills completed and refined (after Wills crashed the first one) was a success to the extent that it generated enough sales and capital to provide for the next Wills-designed car. Ford's main competitor was the nation's top-selling car, the *Curved Dash Olds* of the **Olds Motor Company**. The 1903 **Ford** *Model A* was initially to be called the *Fordmobile*, and early advertising identified it as such.

There were 1,750 *Model A*s made at the Mack Avenue plant in 1903 and 1904. This first car of the **Ford Motor Company** was a different vehicle than the **Ford** *Model A* manufactured from 1927 to 1931. In 1903, sales of the *Model A* put the **Ford Motor Company** on the production charts for the first time. **Ford** was third in automobile manufacturing, behind **Oldsmobile** and **Cadillac**, still led by Henry Leland.

The *Model A* was available in two versions: the two-seater ($750) and the four-seater ($850). The two extra seats were created from an attachment that added a back seat to the vehicle. The two-cylinder engine was located under the seat and drove the rear wheels by chain. The *Model A* contained the Wills planetary transmission, was sold only in red and was advertised as "the most reliable machine in the world."

However, many of the *Model A*s had problems with overheating and slipping transmissions, and the car's top speed was only twenty-eight miles per hour. This was enough of a bad reputation to have customers create the joke, "What do the letters in FORD stand for? Fix or Repair Daily!" The company knew that the next year's model would need major changes to win back the public's approval.

The *Model A* and *Model C* were briefly sold at the same time, although the car immediately following the *Model A* was the *Model B* of 1904, not to be confused with Ford's later *Model B* of 1932. A *Model A* with the larger, ten-horsepower *Model C* engine was also manufactured at the same time and called the *Model AC*.

Coal baron and Ford financier Alexander Malcomson felt that Ford should have a car that would be the high-end model of the company's line, giving **Ford Motor Company** a "luxury car" to offer the public. Although Malcomson had originally hired Ford to produce a low-priced car, the Wills-designed *Model B* was introduced in October 1904. Henry Ford was against putting out the *Model B*, since he was still on a quest to develop the perfect "everyman's car." A luxury car didn't fit into his plans. But Ford needed Malcomson's money, so the company complied.

It took about eight months to get the car and factory tooling ready to manufacture the *Model B*, as it was such a different design than the *Model A*. Assembled in the Piquette Plant, it was an open car and could seat four. It had a larger engine, positioned in front of the driver instead of under the seat. The *Model B* had padded and tufted upholstery, as well as a polished wood body that was painted, according to the advertisements, "a rich dark green." It had brass trim and a brass steering wheel and steering post.

The *Model B* sold for $2,000, as compared to the less-expensive *Model A*. The *Model B*'s four-cylinder engine allowed it to move much faster than the

Early Ford engine designed by Ford and Wills.

46

Model A. It was rated from twenty to twenty-four horsepower, depending on the source. This allowed it to go at a top speed of forty miles per hour. It was manufactured for three years, until 1906, and around five hundred cars were made. It was described in the brochures as a "touring car of light weight and great power."

In the long run, though the *Model B*'s sales figures were respectable and its profit margin acceptable for the times, the stockholders were not overwhelmed. The *Model B* was replaced by the more widely accepted Model F.

The *Model C* made its debut in December 1904 and was by all accounts a vast improvement on the *Model A*. Built in the Piquette plant, it was a two-seater sold as a "doctor's car" and had a top speed of thirty-eight miles per hour. The two-cylinder engine was, however, once more under the seat after being in the front, right behind the radiator, in the previously designed *Model B*. The gas tank was under the hood for the *Model C*. Wills's improvements included a redesigned cooling system; an improved, stronger engine; and a superior transmission. The car was more reliable and handled much better on the road than did the *Model A*. The *Model C* sold for $850, and about eight hundred were made.

The *Model C* targeted doctors in its advertising, extolling its easy handling and increased reliability, since doctors making house calls had to stop and re-start the car many times. Its price was slightly more than the *Model A*, $850 for a runabout and $950 for a covered car (a tonneau). Presumably, a doctor could pay the additional cost, but most people who study Ford history know that Henry wanted to build a car for the masses, not just for doctors.

The variety of models achieved sufficient sales to keep Ford in the top five of auto producers in 1904 and 1905, although it had slipped to number four, behind the **Jeffery Company**'s popular *Rambler*.

The Ford team went through all the letters of the alphabet before stopping with the *Model T*. Not all models were produced. For example, the *Model D* never left the drawing board. A delivery truck was unofficially *Model E*. Other models, such as *G, H, I* and *J*, were Wills-designed prototypes that never made it to the manufacturing stage.

In 1905, the four-seater *Model F* made its debut. It was like the *Model A* and *Model C* but larger and more luxurious. The overall car market had improved, and luxury cars were doing well. As a compromise, Ford brought out the *Model F*, which was a kind of cross between the *Model C* and the *Model B*. Wills retooled the two-cylinder engine with a larger cylinder head and a shorter piston rod. This resulted in a 20 percent increase in the car's horsepower. To help prevent overheating, the car had a larger radiator. Wills took the Dodge brothers' suggestions regarding a longer wheelbase and larger tires. Wills added the first *Ford* running board and a side entrance, providing for easier entry and exit from the vehicle.

An open car and a four-seater with running boards, the *Model F* was built at the Piquette plant, had a green body (an improved paint job from its predecessors) and sold for $1,200. It was meant to bridge the gap between the *Models A* and *B*. The *Model B* was discontinued in 1906 after one thousand were made.

In 1906, Ford introduced the *Model K*, another car meant to appease Malcomson's desire for luxury cars. The *Model K* replaced the *Model B* as the upscale model for the **Ford Motor Company**. The earlier **Ford** models had four-cylinder engines; the *Model K* had six cylinders. In 1907, its second year, it was the best-selling six-cylinder automobile in the world. It could generate forty horsepower and attain speeds of 50 miles per hour. The gas tank was enlarged to hold fifteen gallons, giving the car a range of 250 miles before it had to refuel. The tires and wheelbase had been enlarged, and the axles were fitted with extra ball bearings. On top of that, Wills had supervised the improvement of the *Model K*'s carburetor and ignition system.

The *Model K* had front and rear seats as standard equipment for the first time in a Ford automobile. An optional top and gas lamps were offered. The styling was described as Victorian, with graceful lines and large, roomy, buffed leather seats.

The *Model K* contributed to Ford becoming the number one car company of 1906 and 1907. However, some sources state that the sales figures, although good, were disappointing and not as high as expected.

Malcomson felt the *Model K* wasn't luxurious enough, and plans were made to cease production to build the *Model N*. This, and other incidents, caused Alexander Malcomson to sell his 25 percent of the Ford stock, leaving Henry Ford the majority stockholder. Ford had schemed to get rid of Malcomson because he didn't like being told what he should do with his company. He invented another firm, the **Ford Manufacturing Company**, which included Wills as secretary and totally excluded Malcomson. It would sell parts to the **Ford Motor Company** at an undetermined price. Henry Ford had also formed a dummy corporation that prevented Malcomson from having funds funneled to him.

Before he quit **Ford**, Malcomson decided to announce that he would start his own auto company to build the *Aerocar*, which was advertised as "The Car of Today, Tomorrow, and of Years to Come." This irritated Henry Ford, who hinted that Malcomson might have a conflict of interest and should sell his Ford stock—which he eventually did, after a few irate meetings of the board of directors. The **Ford Manufacturing Company** was dissolved after Malcomson built his own eighty-thousand-square-foot factory to produce his *Aerocar*. This facility stood at Mack Avenue and Beaufait Street, in Detroit, not far from Ford's first factory.

Unfortunately, Malcomson's company went out of business after only about a year, lasting from late 1906 until early 1908. Poor sales for the three different models offered was the reason given for the *Aerocar*'s failure. Malcomson had to sell a lot of coal to recoup his losses, and it took him years to do so. But he still died a multimillionaire.

Meanwhile, the *Aerocar* factory was purchased by J.L. Hudson of department store fame. He needed the factory for the new **Hudson Motor Company**, of which he would be the silent major stockholder. In 1909, **Hudson Motor Company** moved into the *Aerocar*'s old factory to build the first Hudson automobiles.

The *Model K* was advertised to be able to go "Sixty miles an hour—guaranteed!" But sales were slow when the car was priced at $2,500 and even slower when Ford raised the price to $2,800 (the $2,500 price didn't allow for enough profit).

Henry Ford still liked the publicity gained from auto racing and made a racing version of the *Model K* to go on the road and generate publicity. He increased the horsepower from sixty to one hundred. This plan backfired and resulted in bad publicity when Ford lost to J. Walter Christie in a one-on-one race in Daytona Beach, Florida. Ford came in last behind a Fiat, a Darracq (a French auto company) and the Christie race car.

Race-car driver Frank Kulic almost killed himself in a crash in the *Model K* car during a race at the Michigan State Fairgrounds. Consequently, Ford found ways other than racing to promote his vehicles.

J. Walter Christie invented a suspension system widely adapted throughout the industry. The system was one he developed while driving and designing tanks during the Spanish-American War. The suspension system provided longer movement than conventional leaf-spring systems then in use.

He was the first American in the French Grand Prix in 1907 and pioneered front-wheel drive in automobiles, although a prototype race car and five other front-wheel drive cars were all that were manufactured.

However, with the Dodge brothers making the engines, the Wills-designed *Model N* soon went into production. It would draw on the engineering used in the *Model K* and would be an early prototype for the *Model T*.

The *Model N* debuted in January 1906 at the New York Auto Show at Madison Square Garden. This exhibited vehicle was mainly a prototype and a rush job, meant to take advantage of the auto show publicity. Also exhibited were Ford's *Models K* and *F*. These cars would forever replace the *Models A*, *C* and *AC*. **Ford Motor Company** was still selling a backlog of *Model F*s in 1906.

The *Model N* was the first car Wills built with vanadium steel. It had four cylinders, and its engine was in the front. The vehicle sold for $500. It was manufactured from 1906 until 1909, and over 7,000 were made, all of them maroon in color. It was popular because it was rugged and inexpensive. Due largely to the *Model N*'s sales, **Ford Motor Company**'s production for 1906 went up to 8,729, from 1,599 just the year before. This was an overall increase of five and a half times the 1905 numbers.

The *Model N* was a hit, and Henry Ford couldn't make enough of them to meet the public's demand—even when, out of necessity, he had to raise the price to $600. New mass-production methods, the culmination of years of Wills's designing experience and new vanadium steel were keys to the *Model N*'s success. It had four 3-1/4- by 3-1/8-inch cylinders, in pairs and mounted in front, under the hood. The car had fifteen to eighteen horsepower, enabling it to reach forty miles per hour.

The **Ford Motor Company** stayed on top in 1906, 1907 and 1908, producing more cars than its closest competitors **Cadillac**, **Buick**, **Rambler**, **REO**, **Maxwell**, **Studebaker**, **White** and **Oldsmobile**. A major factor that helped keep Ford at the top was the fortuitous encounter Henry Ford had with Walter Flanders.

Walter Flanders had a mechanical brilliance and got his start constructing business machinery for **Singer Sewing Machine Company**. He learned about methods of mass production at Singer, a company that was revolutionary in the evolution of assembly lines. Flanders developed his own methods and began to run his own machine business. He first met Ford while servicing machines he had manufactured—Ford complained to Flanders that the machines he sold him weren't working right. Flanders showed him how to place the machines and adjust them and even taught workers how to use them.

Flanders was then hired by Ford and increased Ford's daily production from six vehicles to twenty, then to twenty-five. **Ford Motor Company** had added a new plant at Bellevue Avenue in Detroit, and Flanders set it up for mass production. He left after two years, in 1908, to form his own car company, becoming the "F" in **E-M-F Motor Car Company**.

Flanders was a large factor in **Ford Motor Company**'s ability to mass-produce automobiles.

In the long run, Flanders's exit was probably best for the teetotalling Ford. Flanders belonged to that large group of automakers, including the Dodge brothers, and sometimes even Wills himself, who were definitely not abstainers. Add Ford's longtime associate Spider Huff to the mix, and it was a disaster waiting to happen. Luckily for Ford and the others, the main harm done was to livers.

In 1907, the Wills-designed *Model R* was introduced. It was a snazzier version of the *Model N*, with a running board, fenders and an oil lamp, features previously available on the *Model F*. Only twenty-five hundred *Model R*s were made from April to October—at that time, a small amount for **Ford**. They quickly sold out. The *Model R*s were red with leather seats and brass fixtures.

Another car similar to the *Model N* was the *Model S*. It came with the option to add a third seat in the back, referred to as a "mother-in-law seat." Other options included gas lamps, a convertible top and an umbrella holder. For the 1907 season, Ford would sell 6,398 *Model N*s and *Model S*s.

On the third story, in the north section and quietest part of the Piquette factory, there was a cordoned-off, secret room. It was the place where the *Model T* was conceived and designed. The *Model T* was what Henry Ford had always wanted to build—a sturdy, reliable and, most important, affordable car for the "common man."

The room was a combination office and drafting room, containing a large blackboard and several drafting tables. During the time that the *Model T* was being designed, per fellow associate Charles Sorenson's book, Wills was "brilliant but high-strung, impatient, and a perfectionist." Sorenson also said that Wills often complained about Henry Ford. Wills felt that his ideas were better than Ford's, and he would attempt to alter Ford's ideas to more closely match his own. Of course, the situation can be attributed to the fact that, by this time, Wills and Sorenson felt thwarted by each other, as both men lobbied for Ford's attention.

After the main work on the *Model T* was complete, Wills began spending less time on development and more time on metallurgy and tool design. He set up a laboratory in the Piquette factory to study steel alloys. In 1908, the year the *Model T* was released, Wills spent much of the year studying and perfecting vanadium steel in the Canton, Ohio metallurgy plant.

By the advent of the Wills-designed *Model T*, each car was still essentially hand-assembled. However, as each model came out, mass production improved a bit, and the price of the vehicle decreased. This was Ford's goal: a car produced at a low enough price that it was affordable for lower-earning families.

After the introduction of the *Model T*, the **Ford Motor Company** doubled and tripled its sales for years afterward, remaining the top-selling automaker the whole time. In 1909, sales went from 10,202 cars to 17,771, then to 32,053 in 1910 and 69,762 in 1911. Following the increase in factory space, sales dramatically soared, from 78,440 in 1912 to 168,220 in 1913 and 308,162 in 1914.

As more cars were produced through mass production, prices went down, making the *Model T* affordable for the "common man," as Henry Ford said. With the improved assembly line and increased manpower, Ford produced more than one million automobiles for the first time in 1921—1,275,618 to be exact.

The *Model T*, also known as the "Tin Lizzie," was so popular that it inspired various side industries providing upgrades to the vehicle. For instance, the Graham brothers' first auto undertaking was to create a kit that would turn a *Model T* into a small truck. They progressed after that to manufacturing trucks. When they sold their truck division to the **Dodge Brothers**, they bought the **Paige-Detroit Car Company** and began to produce automobiles, changing the name to **Graham-Paige Motor Company**. They originally made their money from designing and selling glass jars.

By 1912, the *Model T* had sold more than twelve thousand units and production was relocated from the Piquette plant to a new one in Highland Park, on Woodward Avenue near Seven Mile Road. This was on the first mile of concrete highway in the United States. The road was paved in 1909 on Woodward Avenue, from Six to Seven Mile Road. The concrete highway was eighteen feet wide. Woodward Avenue also had the first modern traffic light and was the start of the Davison Expressway, the first urban freeway.

The great success of the *Model T* allowed Henry Ford to take a trip to Europe. When he returned in 1912, he was appalled and furious that Wills, along with the Dodge brothers, had built a new and improved car to replace the *Model T*. They had retooled machinery for the improved car and even taken advance orders.

But Ford did not want to change what he thought was "the perfect car." He was infatuated with the concept of interchangeable parts, and once the *Model T* proved its popularity with the public, he made it clear he wasn't looking for an "improved" version. To accentuate his point, Ford walked around the prototype Wills and the Dodge brothers had built a few times. Next, he opened the passenger door and yanked it off its hinges! He then went to the other side of the car and repeated the act, tearing off the driver's side doors. He picked up a nearby sledgehammer and proceeded to smash the car to pieces. Witnesses said they had never heard Ford curse before.

Wills thought Ford would be happy that he had been so productive while Ford was gone. What continued to rile Ford was that the factory had already begun to be retooled for the updates Wills had planned. Wills remarked, regarding the incident, that as far as Henry Ford was concerned, "The *Model T* was God and we were to put away false images." Ford later announced that there would be no more improvements to the *Model T*, because it was perfect as it was.

By 1913, the assembly-line method of building automobiles first practiced in the Piquette plant was now being used at the new plant, and production soared. The time it took to build a car went from around twelve hours to ninety minutes, due to this new method of mass production.

In his continuing quest to make the **Ford Motor Company** completely independent, Henry Ford was planning on having the firm manufacture all

Wills and Mabel in another early Ford car, the Model K. Note the crank in front.

Wills married Mary Coyne in 1914. She was the mother of Wills's youngest children, John Harold and Childe Harold Jr.

the parts that were made by other companies. This would be accomplished by the opening of his new River Rouge factory complex, which he started building in 1917. (It would completely open in 1928.)

On January 3, 1914, Harold married Mary Coyne (1883–1975) of New York City, a union that would last until his death. Mary had a daughter, Elaine Pommerer Schenck (1905–1977), from a previous marriage. Together, Harold and Mary had two sons, John Harold (1915–1968) and Childe Harold Jr. (1916–1973). Although C.H. Wills detested the name "Childe," it was evidently not enough to prevent him from giving his youngest son the hated first name. Childe Harold Jr. did not detest the name as much, using it during interviews about his father.

The Dodge brothers, John and Horace, had been one of Ford's major suppliers (and stockholders) since 1902, supplying engines, transmissions and axles. They had manufactured the prototype that Wills designed and Ford destroyed. The brothers took the plans for the prototype that Ford rejected and refined them, producing the first car of the **Dodge Brothers Company**. Wills had developed a lot of innovations for the car, and when

Mabel Wills in an early Ford.

Ford rejected the vehicle plans, Wills patented many of them himself. Wills did well when the **Dodge Brothers Company** licensed his patents for spot welding, all-steel bodies and punch presses. He continued to make a nice side income as other auto companies also licensed his patents.

Although Wills was known as a hard worker, willing to put in long hours, by the time success was bringing him an abundance of wealth, he started spending nights out on the town with the likes of the Dodge brothers. Wills was said to have become "softened by prosperity and high living." Gone were the days when Wills worked one full-time job before heading to his other job. In the old days, he would eat a sandwich on the run and sleep when he could. However, once Wills tasted the **Ford Motor Company**'s success, he began coming in at 11:00 a.m., if at all, and spending more and more time on his yacht. This would eventually lead to a confrontation.

WORLD WAR I INTERVENES

Wills's dissatisfaction with the lack of updates and improvements in the *Model T* took a back seat as the nation entered World War I in 1917. Wills worked with Charles F. Kettering, co-developer of the self-starter and later head of **General Motors**' research department. The company was building the massive, twelve-cylinder, four-hundred-horsepower, V12 Liberty motors for the war effort. Wills met Ralph DeParma, race-car driver, while working on the engines. Wills would later become more involved with DeParma's company.

The plant maintained a high level of production due to Wills's skill in finding the materials, developing the manufacturing methods and designing efficient tooling to produce the needed engines. Wills developed an efficient process to produce engine cylinders using welded tube steel. Members of the **Packard**, **Cadillac**, **Marmon** and **Lincoln** auto companies assisted in developing the Liberty engines. Almost four thousand of the engines were built and sold to Britain and France in 1918.

In April 1917, Wills was also involved in a top-secret project with Kettering, Ford, Elmer Sperry, Orville Wright and Edward Deeds of **Delco Manufacturing** to design the first cruise missile, code-named the "Kettering Bug," at Kettering's lab in Dayton, Ohio. It was a robotic aircraft designed to carry bombs, one-way only, with the aircraft exploding with the bomb. The prototype had accuracy problems, but the knowledge gained was put to good use elsewhere. The "Bug" was also considered as a weapon in World War II.

Ford and Wills were assigned to build an engine for the Kettering Bug, Sperry was given the self-guidance system to design, and Wright was to design the fuselage. Ford and Wills at first tried a two-cylinder engine, but they had to substitute a four-cylinder power source due to vibrations.

By the spring of 1918, the missile was operable and given to Colonel "Hap" Arnold to implement. However, Arnold took ill on the ship on the way to France, and by the time he was well, the Armistice had been signed and the war was over. Project leader Kettering told the participants not to talk about it, and the secret was kept for years.

6

THE PARTING OF THE WAYS

A fter the war, Henry Ford still didn't want to change the *Model T*. As time went on, Ford could build more of the products "in-house," making the equipment in Ford factories. Henry Ford phased out the other companies he contracted with to build Ford parts, such as the **Dodge Brothers**. Meanwhile, the number of Ford employees grew to more than twenty-six thousand.

In 1916, Henry Ford announced that the company would no longer pay dividends to its stockholders. It was widely believed that Ford made the announcement as retaliation, because John and Horace Dodge, now competitors manufacturing their own auto, were two of the biggest stockholders. After World War I, in early 1919, the brothers sued to get their unpaid stock dividends.

During the litigation, one of the attorneys made the remark that Ford wasn't paying dividends and instead was frittering away the money. He cited as evidence the ridiculously large annual salary paid to Harold Wills. This caused John Dodge to jump to his feet and say, "The salary of Wills is not an issue as he is worth every penny he is receiving." He also said that he considered Wills "the brains of the organization."

Ford lost the case, even though Wills testified on his behalf. Ford had to pay a substantial cash settlement to the Dodge brothers.

Henry Ford didn't want to relinquish any control of the company. He formulated a plan to purchase all of the minority stock in the marketplace. That meant that Ford and his son Edsel could control the company, unhindered by a board of directors.

In Ford's quest to pursue the stock of the smaller shareholders, rumors (perhaps started by Ford to lower the stock price?) circulated that Ford had sold his stock to Colonel Du Pont of **General Motors** for $150 million. Another rumor had Wills and John R. Lee planning on building a car similar to a small Cadillac in the Ford Highland Park plant. The car would be named the *WillsLee*. Yet another rumor was that Ford was starting a new company and planning on selling cars for $250. Whether or not these rumors had an effect, Henry Ford purchased most of the outstanding minority stock at reduced prices.

Wills noticed that as all the **Ford Motor Company** old-timers were disappearing, more autocratic men, subservient to Ford's will, were taking their place. These new men included the quick-tempered Charles E. Sorenson, as well as Harry Bennett, hard-boiled head of Ford's private police force.

By 1918 and 1919, Wills had begun making moves toward his goal of producing the best automobile possible. It was an uncertain time in the Ford Highland Park plant, as Henry Ford began moving the **Ford Motor Company** headquarters to Dearborn. Many of the employees were unsure if they would be asked to make the move to the new headquarters. With confusion in the air, Wills recruited many people from the Ford Highland Park plant for his new project. He rewarded most of them by providing them with the best homes on the St. Clair River in Marysville.

When he wasn't planning his move to Marysville, Wills spent time traveling to Canton, Ohio, to study steel-making methods.

After the war, as the distance between Ford and his onetime right-hand man grew wider, coming between Wills and Ford was Charles E. Sorenson. Sorenson had risen through the ranks, working up from being a pattern maker at the Piquette plant to heading the Ford defense department and serving as a Ford board member. He was known for his hard-driving personality, insensitivity to others and explosive temper. He developed a dislike for Wills and did his best to put a wedge between Ford and Wills over the years. It all came to a head when Ford called Wills into his office on a fateful day in 1919.

Ford told Wills he would have to change his living habits or be let go. According to Sorenson, this included telling him, "Get to work at eight o'clock every morning like the rest of us!" Ford then told Wills to stop giving part of his dividend checks to the other employees. He further told him not to give them jewels and to take back the ones he had already given out. Clearly, the friendship between Wills and Ford was not what it used to be.

Wills, surprised by the tirade, responded by spending even more time out of the office. Following the confrontation, according to Wills's associate Ed Clemett, an employee who followed Wills from the Highland Park plant to the new Marysville project, Harold Wills would appear in the dining room at the Highland Park plant unshaven and unkempt. It was further remarked that the wealthy Wills looked like a fugitive from a chain gang.

Once Wills had decided to make his move and start his own company, he had already recruited many of the people around him to follow him to Marysville. He also was organizing and buying small parts companies in preparation to finally follow his dream to assemble his own automobile. As Wills's situation at Ford diminished and became more tangled, he had already been contemplating his future without Ford and dreams of a car of the future. After Wills met Ralph DePalma, he got involved with **DePalma Manufacturing Company**.

DePalma Manufacturing Company was formed in 1916 by successful race-car driver Ralph DePalma and Detroit's Book brothers. DePalma, victor in more than two thousand auto races, had just won the 1915 Indianapolis 500. He was later inducted into the International Motorsports Hall of Fame as well as the Automotive Hall of Fame, the National Sprint Hall of Fame, the Motorsports Hall of Fame and others.

Wills and his Marysville Land Company partner, John R. Lee. Lee had been the head of the sociological department at Ford and quit the same day as Wills.

The other cosigners of the **DePalma Manufacturing Company** were two of the three Book brothers, Frank and Herbert. (James, the eldest, had died in 1916.) The Book brothers were real estate developers and the maternal grandchildren of tycoon Francis Palms. They were famous for developing the land along Washington Boulevard that their grandfather had left to them. They built the Louis Kemper–designed Book Building, Book-Cadillac Hotel ("Cadillac" had been the previous name of the hotel on that location) and the Book Tower, where Wills had an office.

The Book Tower was going to be accompanied by an eighty-one-story skyscraper, which would have been the tallest office building in the world at that time. But the Great Depression hit, and many Detroit building projects were short-circuited, including the planned second spire to Albert Kahn's Fisher Building.

The **DePalma Manufacturing Company** was formed to build engines "with features of *Peugeot* and *Mercedes*." Also, per its articles of association, "To sell and deal generally in motors, motor cars, aeroplanes, motor boats, accessories, and parts thereof." In the 1918 annual stockholders meeting, C.W. Toles is listed with the Book brothers as a stockholder and Harry S. Warren as a director and shareholder.

In 1919, C. Harold Wills was listed as the majority shareholder with 318 shares, although the Book brothers' combined 430 shares were still a majority. Wills was elected president, and John Lee (Wills's new partner) was listed as a stockholder and new member of the board of directors. The company address was listed as 718 Woodbridge Street, Detroit, Michigan.

The bonds between Ford and Wills had severed officially and completely in March 1919. It was clear to Wills that he would never be able to change Ford's mind on improving the *Model T*'s workmanship. There was also the general upheaval in the company due to the ascendancy of Edsel as president and Henry's purchase of all the **Ford** stock.

On March 19, 1919, Wills officially resigned and asked Ford for his share from the agreement they had. The matter was adjudicated, and Wills was awarded $1,592,128. Wills also left Ford's employ with a fortune in his own patents and stock. As Wills left, Henry Ford voiced concerns that he thought Wills was involved in "shady metal deals." This was most likely because he knew Wills had interest in several steel companies. Wills made over $4,000,000 from his steel investments.

Wills's deals weren't "shady," just shrewd. He used his purchase of the **DePalma Manufacturing Company** to undertake testing and work out design criteria for a new automobile. The company was listed in the *Detroit*

Directory of 1919 as owned by Wills. By the end of the year, it would change names to **Lafayette Motor Company**; on December 11, 1919, the name was changed to the **C.H. Wills Motor Company**.

Resigning the same day as Wills was Ford executive John R. Lee. He would become Wills's partner in his new **Marysville Land Company** pursuit.

Wills released a statement upon leaving Ford: "I am anxious to do something worthwhile, and this seems an opportune time to start."

Wills later remarked that one of his reasons for leaving **Ford Motor Company** was the way he saw Henry Ford treat his old supporters, including the Dodge brothers, James Couzens and even Spider Huff. Many people who were around when Ford was starting out tended to disappear as the company became more and more successful.

Wills, however, was one of the last to go, and Henry Ford would probably not have let him leave so easily had he not been so heavily influenced by Sorenson and Bennett. Per many sources, these two men intensely disliked Wills—and any other person capable of getting Ford's attention besides them. Wills told his son C. Harold Jr. that he figured it was only a matter of time until Ford turned on him, also.

A photo of C. Harold Wills when he was president of the **Wills Sainte Claire Motor Company**.

C. Harold and his second wife, Mary, in their later years, around 1935.

The factory called the Piquette plant is where most of Ford's early cars were developed, including the *Model T*. The plant, in Detroit's "Milwaukee Junction," at Piquette Avenue and Milwaukee Street, was where Ford's version of the assembly line was developed.

The iconic V8 engine of the **Wills Sainte Claire**, showing the overhead cams.

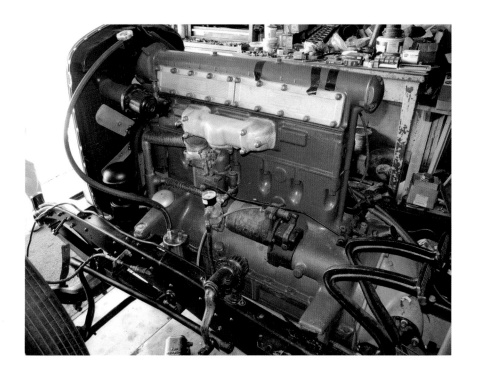

Above: A side view of the **Wills Sainte Claire** six-cylinder engine.

Right: An advertisement for the 1926 **Wills Sainte Claire**. This ad, like most of the Wills auto advertisements, features women. Wills was very receptive to female drivers and realized the value of putting them front and center in his ads. He would show women driving a car, unusual for ads of the day. Many of the car's added attractions, such as lights illuminating the passenger's path as he or she exits the vehicle, were appealing to women. Wills knew that women usually had the last word in a household's auto purchase, and he was happy to appeal to them.

WILLS SAINTE CLAIRE

PLAIN, blunt transportation can be purchased for less than Wills Sainte Claire. There are those, however, who demand and are willing to pay for a plus element called style. And these constitute the Wills Sainte Claire clientele—as they constitute Bendel's and Pierre's.

WILLS SAINTE CLAIRE, INC.
Marysville, Michigan

WILLS SAINTE CLAIRE
The New Vogue Brougham

Strength and lightness, style and generous ease. Excellent coachwork crowning a smart interior.

Its supreme distinction, the distinction of difference—

A car for those who shop in Bond Street, shoot in Scotland and visit the Riviera in March.

WILLS SAINTE CLAIRE, INC.
Marysville, Michigan

Left: This photo was used as a magazine ad for one of the first **Wills Sainte Claires**, the 1922 Roadster. It shows a woman driving the four-passenger Wills Sainte Claire Six sedan. The copy states, "It is the ideal car for the woman to drive."

Below: A 1926 **Wills Sainte Claire** T-6 7-Passenger Sedan, owned by Gary Wurmlinger.

The white 1926 **Wills Sainte Claire** roadster of William Hunsberger. As noted in the original Wills factory newsletter, one could pay fifty dollars extra and select a custom color other than the three generally offered.

A 1924 B-68 **Wills Sainte Claire** 5 Passenger Sedan, owned by the City of Marysville.

Thomas Carmody's **Wills Sainte Claire** 1921 A-68 Roadster.

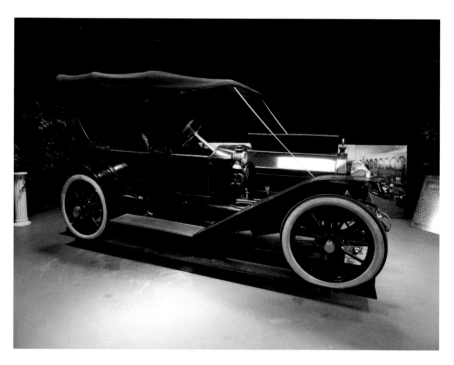

The Havers automobile, built in nearby Port Huron in a factory where the **Northern**, **E-M-F** and **Studebaker** autos were also assembled.

A 1926 T-6 **Wills Sainte Claire** Touring car.

The **Wills Sainte Claire** 1923 A-68 Roadster.

John Porter in a side view of the Harold's Garage section of the Wills Museum.

Publicity shot of the 1926 **Wills Sainte Claire** Roadster owned by Terry and Rita Ernest.

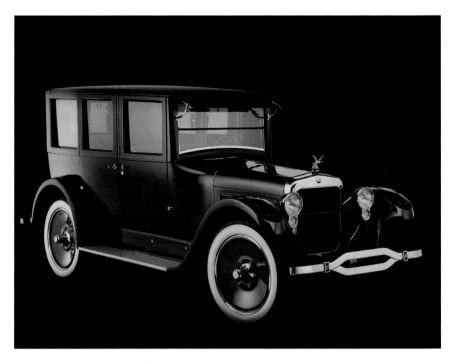

A publicity shot of a brown 1924 Two-Door Brougham **Wills Sainte Claire**.

The 1923 A-68 **Wills Sainte Claire** Roadster of the Stahls Collection in Chesterfield, Michigan.

A greatly accessorized 1922 A-68 **Wills Sainte Claire** touring car, located in the Czech Republic.

A 1926 T-6 **Wills Sainte Claire** Roadster owned by the Henry Ford Museum.

The pictured 1926 T-6 **Wills Sainte Claire** 7-Passenger Sedan is owned by Gary Wurmlinger. Based on the serial number, it is considered to be the newest surviving **Wills Sainte Claire**.

Wills Museum president Terry Ernest in his 1926 T-6 **Wills Sainte Claire** Roadster.

Paul Pawlosky's prize-winning blue 1926 T-6 **Wills Sainte Claire** Roadster.

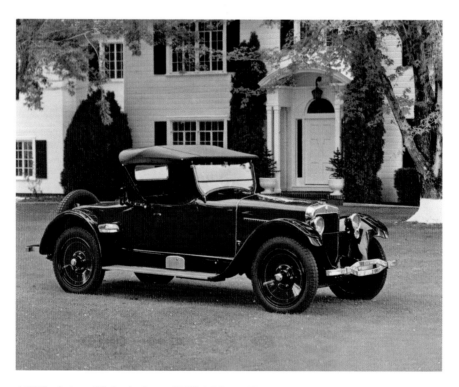

A **Wills Sainte Claire** in front of Wills's Marysville home.

A 1922 A-68 **Wills Sainte Claire** Coupe belonging to Mickey Bascomb and Fred Cleaver. This is the only surviving Wills coupe.

The 1926 T-6 Cabriolet Roadster with a body by Phillips, belonging to Ray Burgess of Port Huron.

The Wills T-6 Touring car of Richard Coulombe from Quebec, Canada.

The **Wills Sainte Claire** Museum exterior in Marysville, Michigan.

Interior shot of the **Wills Sainte Claire** Museum, showing many of the museum's rare autos.

The Transcon Trophy, awarded to L.B. Miller for his record transcontinental run, is pictured, the original of which is in the Wills Museum.

Interior shot of the **Wills Sainte Claire** Museum.

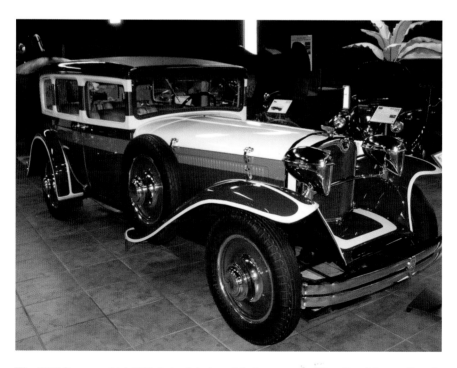

The 1929 Ruxton, which Wills helped design while he sat on the **New Era Motors** Board of Directors.

7

PLANNING THE NEW CAR COMPANY

W hen Wills left **Ford Motor Company**, he didn't waste any time getting his own auto company plans moving. He rented an office in the Book Tower from the Book brothers at 1265 Washington Boulevard, in downtown Detroit. Wills partnered with former Ford associate John R. Lee to form the **Marysville Land Company**.

Wills had discovered the area of Marysville when sailing on his yacht as he was seeking shelter from a storm in a cove nearby. Later, in March 1919, with barely enough time for the ice to have melted, Wills and Lee viewed the area from one of Wills's powerboats.

In 1919, Marysville was not yet even incorporated as a village. As one journalist reporting on the new Wills factory said, the only way most people knew of Marysville was as the interurban railroad stop before Port Huron.

When Wills and Lee formed the **Marysville Land Company** in 1919, they purchased forty-two hundred acres, including four and a half miles of waterfront on the St. Clair River. The area was conveniently serviced by roads, river transportation and railroad. The land, said Wills, had a "natural gradual drainage slope."

The mass media of the day got wind of something going on. When interviewed in 1919, Wills responded and revealed his plan to build a plant and his philosophy on auto manufacturing. He said, "We are not seeking publicity. We are working on our project, and whenever something has reached the point where the news is worthwhile, when it will be of interest, it will be forthcoming. The only thing I will say is that we shall endeavor to place upon the market an automobile that will be found to be as good as it can conscientiously be made. We will start on a big scale, but we expect to become bigger, and that cannot be achieved unless the manufacturer's product is a satisfactory product. So, we shall try to satisfy the public to the best of our ability, and we shall rely on this 'satisfied public' to build up our house."

Wills's announcement set off a land boom in the area. As news of the new plant to be built reached the public, fortune hunters attempted to take advantage. Real estate agents started selling the land at inflated prices. Two Detroit realty firms had their licenses suspended, and two others were reprimanded by the Michigan State Board of Realtors for misrepresentation. The executives of the Wills-Lee Company had reported them for claiming that land they were selling was in the corporate limits of Marysville and near the new Wills-Lee automobile plant when, in fact, it wasn't; the land was miles away from the factory site.

The excitement of a new auto plant had an impact on the Port Huron newspapers. Subtitles to the article included, "Many Plants Coming" and "Big Plant to Locate on the St. Clair River Just South of City [Port Huron]." Another subtitle read, "Millions to Be Spent Here by Men Well-Known in the Financial World." The article went on to relate the positive aspects of the St. Clair River area, including the "Handy Bros. Road," the proximity of the Grand Trunk and Pere Marquette Railroad lines, the Detroit & Cleveland Steam Navigation Company steamers, the White Star Line (a tourist line) and lake freighters of the St. Clair River. Also mentioned was the availability of the Rapid Railway, a suburban railroad called the "Interurban," which had a line running from Detroit to Port Huron. Marysville was not far from the other industrial car cities of Detroit and Flint.

Wills gave another reason for his choice of Marysville—it was far enough from the congestion of Detroit, yet close enough to be easily accessible to the advantages of the Motor City. The fact that there were plenty of woods and wildlife to hunt didn't hurt, either.

8

THE MODEL CITY
OF MARYSVILLE

W ills had decided to build a futuristic city in the area associated with his car factory. In a 1919 interview with the *Detroit Free Press*, he called his proposed Utopia the "city of contented living," as well as "the dream city." Other occasional slogans used were "Marysville, the city of contented homes" and "We live and build in Marysville." He felt that workers who were well paid, contented and decently housed would work better, take more pride in their work and, consequently, build a better car. He thought that if he provided the right environment, workers would be at their best.

Wills wished to educate his workers in all facets of the car they were building, hoping to instill pride in their work. He also wanted them to be able to learn one another's jobs to increase interest and relieve boredom.

EARLY DAYS OF MARYSVILLE

The area where he bought land was in St. Clair County, near a settlement that began in 1786 on Bunce Creek. In 1843, Edward Vickery bought land from Cummings Sanborn and built a sawmill. The settlement began to be known as Vickery's Landing, then Vicksburgh. On April 24, 1844, the post office from nearby "Mack's Place" was moved to the hamlet; Ed Vickery became the postmaster.

Mack's Place was the general store of former Detroit mayor Andrew Mack, who had also been a sea captain. Mack had sailed around the world three times, cofounded the *Detroit Free Press* and had been a colonel in the War of 1812. Mack Avenue in Detroit (where Ford's first factory was located) was named for Andrew Mack (1780–1854).

Mack bought a sawmill that had been built by partners known only as Meldrum and Park. When they built the mill, the creek was known as Meldrum's Creek. After they sold the mill to Andrew Mack, the creek became known as Mack's Creek. As he ran the post office from his general store, Mack's Place became a center of commerce for the area.

When Mack died in 1854, the post office was transferred to Vicksburgh. Because another post office shared that name in Michigan, in 1858, the name of the post office was changed to honor the wife of the man who had taken over the sawmill, Nelson Mills. Mills was the new owner of the mill, and his wife's name was Mary—in 1855, Vicksburgh became Marysville. Early Marysville had its heyday in the early 1900s, when Nelson Mills had three mills. Marysville then went into a decline in 1904 when Mills died, until 1919, when Wills announced his new plant in Marysville.

When incorporated as a village, the name Marysville was kept, since Mary was also the name of C. Harold Wills's wife. Some early jokes said that Wills had chosen the town due to its having the same name as his wife, Mary Wills, and his mother.

While at first Wills's dreams had been built around manufacturing a superior automobile at an affordable price, his ideas expanded into building a model district where his workers could live. This community or "company town" would be built close to his production facilities.

The phrase "company town" at one time conjured up mining and lumber towns, where the "company store" was the only resource in the middle of the wilderness to get supplies, often with "script" issued by the company instead of money and good only at the company store.

Wills was not the first to build "model communities" in the early 1900s. Two other examples of industrialists trying to apply their own brand of idealism in starting a company town include Milton S. Hershey, whose town in Hershey, Pennsylvania, can still be viewed as a tourist attraction, and George Pullman. In 1880, Pullman, builder of luxury railroad cars, constructed a company town near Chicago that he named Pullman.

Thinking that providing a Model Town would prevent worker discontent, George Pullman refused to negotiate when his dissatisfied workers did the unthinkable and went on strike. The strike had a ripple effect that eventually shut down the whole railroad system. The Model Town unraveled. Today,

The first streets of one of the first single-family houses built for the Wills complex is pictured.

the ninety row houses of Pullman's employee housing are in the National Historical Register.

One of the first company towns that attempted to achieve a better environment for workers was the textile town of Lowell, Massachusetts, in the 1820s. A similar community was Steinway Village in the Queens borough of New York, inhabited by the workers who built pianos there. The village had its own amusement park and streetcar line, linking the residents to the rest of New York.

In many cases, as in Marysville, the newly constructed company towns would include parks and common buildings, as well as "modern conveniences" of the day, including indoor bathrooms and running water. Other forms of infrastructure included sewers, streetlights, roads and sidewalks. Many figured that building towns would be more cost effective than dealing with labor unions, although Wills appears more than most to have been altruistic toward the workers he assigned to the assembly line. Wills hoped that Marysville would be "a city without poverty, without social unrest, and without slums."

Since John Lee had enforced the moral codes set up by Henry Ford, there were fears that this would happen in Wills's town. But such fears never materialized. Although Wills tried to construct his model city, he didn't try to control the lives of his workers.

Henry Ford took a shot at developing his own company towns, starting in 1936, about eighteen years after the beginning of Wills's town. Although no doubt influenced by Wills's ideas, Ford's own towns leaned more toward the company store idea than the utopian.

Ford's town of Alberta, Michigan, a company town he constructed in the Upper Peninsula, included an interesting feature. The sawmill in Alberta (one of seven Ford built in the Upper Peninsula to meet the lumber needs of his auto empire) was self-sufficient, running on its own waste. Conveyor belts would take the sawdust and the branches that did not make the cut and direct them right back to the fire powering the sawmill. The mill, besides cutting lumber, also provided the electricity for the village. Ford had a house in Alberta and would spend time there with Clara.

A little-known fact about Ford is that he is credited with inventing the charcoal briquette as a way to get rid of the wood ashes from his auto factory. With the ashes hardening to crushed charcoal, Ford had the crushed charcoal mixed with a potato starch glue and then fashioned into the familiar charcoal briquette shape. Ford and his cousin E.G. Kingsford

The community houses for single men were built first. If workers were laid off, they weren't charged rent while they were out of work. If they had fewer hours, the rent was reduced accordingly.

formed a company to sell them, called Ford's Iron Mountain Plant. The company was later renamed for Kingsford.

Wills studied all the best features of other model industrial communities in his quest to build his perfect town. Among the basic rules he followed were that the streets had to be at least 60 feet wide and one-third of the community's area had to be devoted to "parks, playgrounds, and boulevards." Wills's model city was planned to include not only schools, churches and parks but also housing on lots 40 feet wide by 120 feet long— "large enough to have a vegetable garden." Each house was equipped with an electric stove.

Growth of Marysville

Lee and Wills invested $3.5 million to build Marysville's infrastructure, including municipal buildings, playgrounds, roads and utilities. In total, seventy-five engineers were hired to plan the town and hundreds more to build it. Sewers were constructed, water mains laid and electric lights installed.

To accommodate single men, there would be ten "community houses." Each structure was designed for sixty men. There would later be an area in Marysville composed of housing for employees of the Morton Salt Company called the "Salt Block," assuring that Wills's idea stayed alive in the city. A large community center was built.

Wills and his family moved into a house at 128–29 River Road in Marysville and continued to maintain a Detroit home at 8344 Jefferson Avenue. At one point, their Jefferson Avenue home was robbed. The news hit the Detroit papers, one article mentioning that two caretakers were the only ones in the house at the time.

As the **Marysville Land Company**, John R. Lee planned the incorporation of the village and platted a residential area with 2,881 lots for workers' homes. Marysville was incorporated as a village on September 17, 1919, and incorporated as a city in 1924.

The *Detroit Free Press* took notice of the "city of contented workers," the motto popularized by the Wills people. The *Free Press* ran a special section on the project as it progressed, noting that the community houses being built for unmarried workers "rival many college dormitories in comfort and appearance." Also noted were the common dining hall, which could seat four hundred men, and the fine appearance of the houses reserved for married couples. The article noted the progress on the factory as it was being built,

The community center for Marysville was completed in just one day.

The factory construction continued as the "model city" was built.

including the number of workers soon to be employed, housed and fed by the new auto company.

Although the winter of 1918–19 was one of Michigan's worst to date, the work on the Model Town continued unabated. At one point, the builders were adding one house per day, as reported by the *Port Huron Times Herald*. An auditorium, or community center, seating twelve hundred people was erected in a single day. The auditorium was used for movies and theatrical entertainment for the employees.

COMMUNITY RELATIONS

Wills and his new company did a lot to endear themselves to the townspeople. Wills gave a bank account to every child in Marysville and held a circus for the whole town. In the razing of structures to build the new community, Wills left the Methodist Episcopal church as a historic reminder of the town's existence was before Wills came.

Associations sprang up in the new locality, among them the Half-Shell Club, named for the half shell, the *q* symbol for open and aboveboard, square dealing. (The inference was that an "unworthy" oyster is readily discovered on the half shell.)

The influence that Wills and his factory had on the community is typified by the Minor family. Five Minor brothers all worked in the **Wills** factory. Albert balanced cranks and Jed cut gears. Earl, Jack and Wellington worked in the tool-grinding department.

Earl went on to grind cylinders on the V8 and six-cylinder **Wills** engines and became one of the workers responsible for the "accuracy, precision, and close tolerances" that the **Wills** vehicles became known for. **Ford Motor Company** and **Lincoln** workers would come by to look at the Wills process and its renowned precision.

The construction of the town infrastructure and the **Wills** factory drew attention from other business concerns that wished to take advantage of a great opportunity. Six other manufacturing firms were reported by the *Free Press* to have asked Wills if they could purchase land in the new community. The first company to follow through was the Edison Company. It spent $2.5 million to build a plant to provide gas and electricity to the fledgling town.

To lure more industries to Marysville, a full-length motion picture was made and shown all around the state. The *Bad Axe*, a Michigan newspaper, included an ad for the movie about Marysville, stating that it would be

The factory, once completed, was one of the most modern car factories of the day.

The employees of the **Wills Sainte Claire** plant gather for a photo.

screened for free at the Bad Axe Opera House. The film shows views of the new Detroit Edison plant, the American Brushings plant and the Transeau-Williams Drop Forge site, which would house the largest plant in the world making forgings. Also in the film was the **Illinois Tool Company** factory, which provided the *Wills Sainte Claire* factory's tooling. Two other businesses in the film were the **Aluminum Manufacturing Plant** site, another Wills supplier, and the **Athol Manufacturing Company**, which made upholstery. The film showed the factory of the **C.H. Wills Motor Company** as well as the plant of the Morton Salt Company.

The title of the film was *A Free Trip to Marysville—by Motion Picture*. The cinematographer was C.L. Jacobson, who had a lot of experience shooting **Ford Motor Company** promotional and documentary films. The film showcased the building of the Wills factory and other construction in the growing village. Pictured were vignettes of daily life in Marysville, including, as an article in the *Port Huron Times Herald* stated, the foremen, mechanics, engineers, carpenters and the ditch diggers. Other scenes showed empty, cleared land ready for industry, as if the point that this was a booming area hadn't already been made. The movie was shown for free all across Michigan.

In 1919, Wills and Lee purchased 225 acres that was part of a Native American reservation in Sarnia, Ontario, across the river in Canada. Wills attended a meeting at the Indian Council of the Reservation. He explained that, when needed, the company planned to build a factory on the land it had purchased. Wills promised that any plant built would hire Native Americans. Wills & the **Marysville Land Company** paid $50,000 for the land and promised to build a better road and construct proper drainage facilities.

The Wills and Lee concerns also purchased the Sandusky brickyards that were located on the outskirts of Marysville. Plans were to increase production fourfold, from ten thousand to forty thousand bricks a day.

Prior to the opening of the Wills plant, the *Port Huron Times Herald* and the *Detroit Free Press* had given the Wills operation generous free publicity. The *Times Herald* especially prolonged the publicity. With great fanfare, it ran multipage articles describing the opportunities the auto plant brought to the Port Huron area. Throughout Michigan's long auto history, Port Huron had been largely left out, having had only minor forays into the burgeoning auto business.

Port Huron had seen the exit from the city of the **Anderson Carriage Company**, which reemerged in Detroit as the **Detroit Electric Car Company**, one of the longest-lived electric car companies, operating until 1939.

In 1907, Port Huron was also home to a factory of the **Northern Manufacturing Company**, later called the **Northern Motor Company**. The company was started by Charles Brady King, the first man to drive a car on the streets of Detroit in 1896; Jonathan Maxwell, whose later company, the **Maxwell Motor Company**, was the forerunner of **Chrysler**; and Charles Palms, grandson of Francis Palms, at one time the richest man in the Midwest. They opened a factory in Port Huron in 1907 to build the company's two-cylinder version of the *Northern*. The four-cylinder version was built in Detroit, as was the company's first car, the one-cylinder *Northern Runabout*. The car was promoted as being the "Silent Northern," which was "Dustless and Noiseless."

In 1909, **E-M-F Motor Car Company** absorbed the **Northern Motor** and **Wayne Motor Companies**. The Port Huron factory was then used to build the *E-M-F* automobile. **E-M-F** was later absorbed by the **Studebaker Corporation**, and the factory was used to build *Studebakers* for a short time.

In 1911, the Havers brothers acquired the factory from **Studebaker** to build the well-regarded and well-built *Havers* automobile. The company ceased production in 1914 when the factory burned down, and the Havers brothers did not rebuild. A *Havers* auto, owned by the Wills board president, is one of the vehicles often exhibited in the Wills Sainte Claire Museum.

As the St. Clair County area was finally getting some of the lucrative auto action that was making Detroit so successful, there was a great deal of celebration when the cornerstone to Wills's factory was laid in mid-November 1919. Attending the ceremony were many dignitaries, including Michigan governor Albert E. Sleeper, a popular two-term governor whose tenure coincided with World War I. He sponsored legislation creating the Michigan State Park system, Michigan's first separate labor department, the Michigan State Police, a county road system and, notably, the first state driver's licenses.

9

THE C.H. WILLS COMPANY

The company name was the **C.H. Wills & Company**. Wills spent 1920 planning and building his factory (and village), meticulously working out every detail. Wills and Lee closed the "Wills-Lee" office in Detroit's Book Building in September and moved most of its operations to a separate area in the Marysville plant. The operations that hadn't made the move yet, including the purchasing department, were moved to the **DePalma Manufacturing** building on Woodbridge Street in Detroit.

The name of the car to be built was the *Wills Sainte Claire*—"Wills," after the founder, and "Sainte Claire," for the St. Clair River. Wills added the *e*'s to St. Clair because he thought it looked classier.

According to Charles Sorenson, in his account of his years with Ford, in 1920, the Fords were on their yacht taking a trip up the river to Lake Huron when Sorenson pointed out the new Wills plant. Ford said, "Why not stop and see Wills?"

A phone call was put to Wills, and the yacht was docked at a nearby pier. Wills came aboard and talked for about an hour and showed Ford and the others on the yacht a blueprint of his new V8 engine. Sorenson noted that the overhead valve engine and the drive to the overhead camshaft was driven by a train of gears from the crankcase. Sorenson felt the engine was too complicated and different from the simple L-head engine of the *Model T*. He felt, and was proved right, that the engine was too difficult for most mechanics to work on.

But this didn't bother Wills, who went on to insinuate that he preferred the more complicated way of doing things than the "simplicity" of Ford. The group pleasantly chatted on Ford's boat for more than an hour before parting ways. This is the last recorded time Wills saw or talked to Ford.

In the meantime, in December 1920, Mr. and Mrs. Wills threw a Christmas party for the people of Marysville. Wills gave every schoolchild in Marysville their own gift! The gift was hung on the giant Christmas tree and had each child's name on it.

Harold and Mary Wills always felt a paternal affection for the townspeople of Marysville. For instance, when labor hours were cut due to low auto sales, Harold made sure that rents in the Marysville housing area were lowered accordingly. If a man was given half his usual hours, the rent would be cut in half. If he was laid off completely with no hours, nothing was owed for that month's rent.

Since his days with Ford, Wills knew the value of publicity in establishing racing records. On August 17, 1921, he decided to do something to prove the durability and quality of the *Wills Sainte Claire* and to increase sales. Wills chose a car fresh off the assembly line and set out with a few friends to personally drive the 1921 model on a run from Detroit to New York.

They took the Canadian route, going through Niagara Falls, and covered the whole 689 miles in a record-breaking twenty hours and twenty-six minutes. The car ran fine; the only problems on the trip were a flat tire and some poor-quality gasoline that had to be bled out of the system.

Wills then did a run from New York to Boston and back. The round-trip took eleven hours and forty-seven minutes. These were remarkable runs for the day, as the roads were still very primitive.

After the record runs, the New York Company of Wills Sainte Claire sold most of its cars and was now taking advance orders.

B.E. Smith drove a *Wills Sainte Claire* from New York to Montreal, a distance of 804 miles, in June 1922. The director of the New York State Motor Vehicle Bureau admonished the effort: "You must well know that this is a violation of the State law in regard to speed, as you must have made more than 50 to 60 miles an hour at times in making this run, and it would appear that the driver could hardly have maintained a safe rate of speed through villages and built-up communities." This did not hurt the *Wills Sainte Claire*. Wills had stated in early advertising that the car could accelerate from two miles per hour to seventy miles per hour in high gear.

The **C.H. Wills & Company** vice-president, E.F. Miltenberger, enthused: "Such extraordinary achievements are not merely establishing records; they are demonstrating that for stamina, for endurance, for safety, and ease of driving, the Wills Sainte Claire is without precedent or parallel in motor transportation. These are concrete accomplishments of Molybdenum steel and advanced engineering."

In 1922, the *Wills Sainte Claire* joined new cars at the New York Auto Show, along with other company newcomers, **Durant** and **Rickenbacker Motor Company**. The 1922 *Wills Sainte Claire*, also labeled *Model-68*, was available in several models: a touring model that could seat five passengers; a roadster and a coupe, which seated four; and a sedan, limo and town car, all of which could accommodate seven passengers. The autos used the V8 overhead cam engine, which generated sixty-seven horsepower. The wheelbase was 121 inches.

From the beginning, the cars were built of molybdenum steel, a more advanced form of the vanadium steel that Wills had revolutionized in the use of in Ford's *Model T*. Wills's car would be the first to use his new metal. Molybdenum is created by combining molybdenite with steel. This makes a very strong alloy that is more corrosion-resistant. The material has increased toughness, improved machinability and a greater resistance to high temperatures. In addition, it intensifies other alloying elements. Molybdenum steel was used for all the crankshafts, cams and rods in the *Wills Sainte Claire*. The process was discovered by German military equipment manufacturers during World War I.

Another Wills innovation was an automobile engine inspired by the eight-cylinder *Hispano-Suiza* aero engine, used in airplanes during World War I. The engine had a similar twin overhead camshaft and was constructed with a one-piece cylinder head and block construction in the style of the plane engine. The sleek body lines and lower center of gravity were additional similarities. Wills customized it by substituting spiral bevel gears for the straight bevel gears used in the original design. It was the first use of an overhead cam V8 engine in a car. The downside to this modern engine was that most mechanics of the day didn't know how to fix it.

Wills acquired his *Hispano-Suiza* in 1919, after he stopped working for Ford, probably because Henry Ford would yell at anyone who wasn't driving a Ford car—right before he fired them.

Wills had a molybdenite mine he had purchased in Climax, Colorado. This was 1918, as Wills began planning his own car company. The molybdenite mine was the largest in the United States, and Wills used it to his advantage. The molybdenum steel would help the car stand

The Wills family, including Mary Wills and the two boys, is shown in an Italian vehicle, the Hispano-Suiza. The car was an inspiration to Wills when he planned his own car. The chauffeur is also shown. *Photo by C. Harold Wills Sr.*

continuous stress without fatigue. It's likely that no one had studied or was more knowledgeable in the use of industrial steel than Wills.

Wills, in fact, held so many patents on steel that he purportedly had the steel car itself patented. To avoid paying a royalty to Wills, other auto manufacturers would be sure something in their car was wooden, to avoid having a car that was "all steel."

Using his inexpensive molybdenum source, Wills's first *Wills Sainte Claire Model A-68* used molybdenum steel for the crankshaft, camshaft, springs, front axle, gearbox gears and shafts, connecting rods, propeller shaft, steering knuckles and wheels, and the frame.

The **C.H. Wills & Company** factory was fully built and operable for manufacturing automobiles with an overhead cam V8 engine by January 1921. However, the first car didn't roll off the assembly line until later that spring, in March. Wills was committed to having his automobile be as fine a car as could be built, even if it cost six times as much as the Ford *Model T* (which it did).

Wills would not let any car leave the factory until he was satisfied it was the best it could be. Unfortunately, the car lost out on advance orders when people cancelled their orders due to the car being so delayed. Later, customers waited at the factory for their cars to come down the assembly line, where Wills himself would often check them over.

The first *Wills Sainte Claire Model A-68* was a roadster model considered ahead of its time. It had the features later associated with Wills cars: the overhead cam engine and Hill-start Assist Control (HAC).

Salesmen would often show up at the factory, including one selling steering wheels he claimed were indestructible. Wills jumped on it, and it came apart, with pieces flying in all directions. The salesman didn't even bother picking up the pieces; he just turned and ran.

Other inspirations garnered from the *Hispano-Suiza* included a long hood and a vertical windshield with two glass panes, an extra engine oil reservoir below the left cowl, electric headlamps, an oil pan below the frame and rear brakes. These were just a few of the features that the first *Wills Sainte Claires* and the *Hispano-Suiza* had in common.

Completed **Wills** autos, in a row. They have covers to protect the paint from dirt and stones during delivery. Locals said the covers were to protect the car from goose droppings.

The radiator of the **Wills Sainte Claire** auto, with its goose head ornament.

The interior of the **Wills Sainte Claire** roadster.

The car was announced before enough were built to take advantage of the announcement. Initially, production was slated to begin in August 1920, with ten thousand autos costing $2,000 apiece to be manufactured. Instead, it wasn't until March 1921 that any cars appeared, and the price had risen to $3,000.

The car was considered a luxury model by the time Wills finished his improvements. He wanted to release only the best cars possible, so most "accessories" were standard. The automobile's standard features included an ammeter, demountable wheels and rims, an electric horn, theft locks, a toolkit with high-quality tools, a Zenith duplex carburetor, a single-unit starter/generator, windshield wipers, a single-key locking system for the ignition and a spare-tire carrier.

The *Wills Sainte Claire* also had an engine fan, tilting ("Mirro-Tilt") headlights that were controlled from the steering column and a full-pressure engine lubrication system. There was a sidelight, patented by Wills, which would illuminate the passenger's entry and exit. It could also be used to provide light for nighttime tire repairs. Even though Wills's original vision included building a $2,000 car that everyone could afford, the reality was a $3,000 car considered more of a luxury automobile.

Although it was the first year for the car, the 1921 *Wills Sainte Claire* had a full complement of body types. The wheelbase chassis size was 121 inches and, in later models, 127 inches. The touring model was painted Huron Blue and sold for $2,475. There was a roadster that came equipped with a rumble seat. It was available in a variety of colors—Lady Mary Maroon, Newport Blue and Liberty Green—and sold for $2,575. Those were the open body types. There were several "closed cars," and they came in Fisher Blue, Brewster Green, black or maroon. The four-passenger coupe sold for $3,275, the sedan for $3,475 and the Imperial Sedan was $100 more at $3,575. A brougham was offered at $3,375, and limousine or town car models sold for $3,850.

The Wills factory manufactured and assembled most of the mechanical parts for the *Wills Sainte Claire*, because C. Harold preferred to concentrate on the mechanics and purchase the exterior bodies from many of the body manufacturers of the day. These would be built per Wills's specifications. He used most of the body companies in business at the time, including **Budd Manufacturing Company**, **Babcock**, **Baker**, **Fisher Brothers**, **Willoughby**, **Erdman-Guider**, **Gotfredson**, **Witham** and **American**.

The 1921 and 1922 *Wills Sainte Claire* autos were the first cars to have a dial on the steering column to switch from bright to dim headlights and back-up lights that went on automatically when the car was put in reverse. Wills often backed into fire hydrants in the dark, which was one of the reasons he added back-up lights. The 1925 and 1926 *Wills Sainte Claire* cars had belts to drive the water pump cooling system, with a fan to cool the engine that would use a fan clutch to shut off when not needed. The generator and fan were driven from the gear case, eliminating the need for a fan belt.

Other *Wills Sainte Claire* innovations included an automatic spark advance and a single-unit starter generator system. It was known as the "Molybdenum Car" for the metal used throughout the vehicle. Precise spiral bevel gears cut down on engine noise. Advertising for the car made mention of the Stone Age, Bronze Age, Iron Age, Steel Age and Alloy-Steel Age. Now, the ad stated, the world was entering the Molybdenum Age!

As commendations about the car came in, the staff, which included more than five hundred workers, began to feel a glow of pride and became, like Wills, conscientious in their work. For instance, a letter from Fred Duesenberg of the highly regarded **Duesenberg Auto and Motors Company**, wrote to Wills: "I have had most excellent service out of this car. It has now been run 4,400 miles and I have given it considerable and hard service, but find it a very convenient car to get around in, easy to drive, easy to start, and absolutely free from trouble. I certainly wish you every success, as I feel the whole company deserves it, and I want to take this opportunity of thanking you for the excellent manner in which you have looked after my job."

Another notable letter was reprinted in an auto magazine of the day, *Automobile Topics*, in August 1921. It related how a man from Michigan had gone to Ohio in his *Wills Sainte Claire* before it had been properly tuned. He stopped at an Ohio Wills dealer, and they fixed it right away, no charge. He then got hit by a wayward driver in Dayton. The Wills dealer that he took it to in Dayton even helped him collect insurance money from the man who had hit him. They told the customer that *Wills Sainte Claire* owners watched out for each other, and they considered a fellow Wills owner like a brother.

Other famous *Wills Sainte Claire* owners included Edward Budd of the **Budd Company**, which made bodies for some of the Wills autos; Elizabeth Arden, the original cosmetics queen, who was a close friend of Mary Wills; the Book brothers; silent movie star Conrad Nagel; and Virginia Briggs, daughter of Walter O. Briggs, the Detroit Tigers' owner, of **Briggs Body Company** fame. Famed *Saturday Evening Post* artist Norman Rockwell, Mrs. Horace Dodge of the **Dodge Brothers**, Henry Stetson of the Stetson Hat Company and J.D. Wooster of Lambert Pharmaceuticals all owned *Wills Sainte Claires*.

Frank Willard, creator of the popular comic strip *Moon Mullins*, sent to Wills a cartoon of Moon and Mushmouse riding in a *Wills Sainte Claire*. Henry Ford purchased a 1926 *Wills Sainte Claire* Roadster for his niece. He apparently didn't harbor dark feelings about Wills forever.

The car was considered by many to have the best V8 engine available. Other companies with V8 engines at the time included **Apperson**, **Cadillac**, **Cole**, **Cunningham**, **Daniels**, **Duesenberg**, **Kenworthy**, **King**, **Lafayette**, **Lincoln**, **Oldsmobile**, **Parenti**, **Peerless**, **Standard** and **Wharton**.

Unlike the days when Henry Ford chided Wills about coming in at the late hour of 11:00 a.m., once Wills had his own auto company, it restored his work ethic. He would be at the plant at 2:00 a.m. if he had an idea and would spend the next twelve hours working on it. One interviewer found him in the plant in the middle of the night, wearing a stethoscope and listening to the timing gears. His typical outfit comprised corduroy trousers, a wool shirt and high leather boots, typical of the "working president" he was. He could be found in the drafting room, the plant, the machine shop, the lab or outdoors helping to conduct road tests of the Wills cars. The only place he usually couldn't be found was in his office.

Wills's yacht caught fire while tied up at the Marysville Docks on the St. Clair River. This was not long after he had started his car factory in Marysville. The yacht was eight years old, 140 feet long and one of the few with a diesel engine. It was originally built as a steam yacht for Alexander Winton of the **Winton Car Company**.

Wills was sleeping on the yacht when he was awakened at 3:00 a.m. by the sounds of the fire crackling. In his pajamas, he awakened the other four men on the ship (a mate, steward, chief engineer and Japanese valet). By the time they reached the deck, the entire yacht was enveloped in flames. The other four men jumped to a nearby small dock. Wills got separated and jumped over the side of the boat. Wearing a life jacket, he hung on to the stern of the boat until rescued by a passing motorboat. The boat sank before the eight hundred gallons of gasoline and nearly fourteen hundred gallons of fuel oil could explode. The loss was estimated at $150,000, although Wills stated that some of it was covered by insurance. Unstated in those Prohibition days was the fact that the cargo included a very large storehouse of whiskey.

Wills's chosen emblem for the car, the "Gray Goose," represented the Canada geese Wills had long admired migrating from the north to their winter homes in the south. He called the Gray Goose the "wisest, freest, traveler of the skies" and felt it represented abundant trees and water in Marysville. The logo went on all *Wills Sainte Claire* autos as a radiator ornament.

The hood ornament's nickel-plated pewter goose was designed by Irving Florman. The 1921 model depicted the goose with its wings down. From 1923 to 1926, a "wings-up" goose was used to differentiate it from the *Hispano-Suiza*'s stork ornament when legal action was threatened.

Wills used a test track in unsettled land about two miles from his factory to give the cars a test run. He would drive up sandy hills, down into a pit, then up onto solid ground, all to test the endurance of the cars and to see how they would fare on the substandard roads of the day.

The sales force for the *Wills Sainte Claire* autos were given an education on the car as part of their training. The company newsletter, the *Gray Goose Bulletin*, printed much of this information and all the news of the *Wills Sainte Claire* for auto dealers across the nation. The *Gray Goose* was "published twice a month in the interests of those who build and sell the Wills Sainte Claire," as stated on the masthead.

The *Gray Goose* reported on dealerships in Albany, Syracuse, New York City and Buffalo in New York; Detroit and Grand Rapids in Michigan; Cincinnati and Cleveland, in Ohio; Washington, D.C.; Jacksonville, Florida; Boston, Massachusetts; Pittsburgh and Philadelphia in Pennsylvania; and more. Chicago had four *Wills Sainte Claire* dealerships, serving the four corners of the city.

The newsletter had contributions from all over the nation. A.S. Pawling sent a picture of him driving his *Wills Sainte Claire* up the steps of the New York State Capitol in Albany. He was "on his way to see Governor Al Smith." Pictures showed the *Wills Sainte Claire* being driven in various locales, such as the desert and the woods. Any news about the *Wills Sainte Claire*, such as new speed or endurance records, was prominently featured, as were sales statistics, promotions for the sales staff, sales tips and more.

During his last two years at Ford, 1918 and 1919, Wills wasn't given much to do, so he spent most of his time designing the *Wills Sainte Claire*. By the time he got around to building the car, it had been fully planned in his head.

Most experts agree that of all the positive aspects of the *Wills Sainte Claire*, the advanced engineering of the engine is a highlight. A tall and narrow engine (except the V8), its accessibility was the key, because everything was visible and easy to get to. Therefore, it wasn't always necessary to dismantle the entire engine to access the source of the problem, unlike with most cars.

The camshaft and valve housing and the cylinder head were detachable as one unit. Removing two cover plates on the left side of the camshaft provided easy access to the valves in case they needed adjusting. Changing a piston or bearing was a simple matter of removing the oil pan. Spark plugs could be changed in seconds.

While working for Ford, Wills also had many years to ponder the manufacture of the *Wills Sainte Claire* engine. Thus, every improvement he used was tried and true—Wills didn't have any "experimental features" in his engines. Every engine was assembled using proven engineering and metallurgy. The hundreds of thousands of miles many of these motor cars were driven is proof of their durability. Their preciseness of manufacturing is indicative of the care put into the production of each automobile.

The dominant feature of the Wills motor is the design of the camshaft and overhead valve configuration, eliminating the need for lifters, pushrods, rocker arms, gears, chains and rollers. The lack of rocker arms to open and close valves meant less wear on the engine, so it is less inclined to need service. Eliminating wasted motion increases the efficiency of the engine and makes the need for adjustment less frequent.

The automobile's generator and fan were gear-driven, with a cast-aluminum cooling fan that would disengage at forty-two miles per hour. The thermos-syphon cooling system eliminated the need for a water pump.

Wills's experiments with Liberty aircraft engines and molybdenum steel led him to develop an engine that was lighter but stronger. He used his steel experiments to develop an engine not handicapped by the extra weight that heavier steel would provide.

The car's smaller dimensions mean it has a minimum of inertia to overcome, providing a smooth ride. Wills's patented "steadying device" kept the gears, camshaft and valve mechanisms operating precisely and silently. The balanced balloon tires were also a factor in the smooth ride. The standard Wills tires were the Firestone "Gum Dipped Balloon" tires.

The preciseness of engineering was aided by the more than $300,000 the factory had invested in precision gauges. Perfectionist Wills spared no expense in using the most modern machinery available. The *Wills Sainte Claire* was built to be the best.

Many automobiles of the day were mostly assembled using a variety of manufacturers to provide parts such as carburetors and bodies. However, Wills produced many essential ingredients in-house. The camshaft, valve follower and Wills-patented steadying device were all forged at the plant from the light but strong molybdenum steel. The Wills crankshaft, with dimensions set within one-half thousandth of an inch, and the Wills bearings were known throughout the industry as the best in the business.

The Wills connecting rods were made of an aluminum alloy known as Lynite, causing them to be lightweight but strong and able to reduce stress. Each set of connecting rods was weighed and balanced so that the weight of the rods would not vary more than a small, fractional part of an ounce. This preciseness of manufacturing is what helped free the Wills vehicles from vibrations at any speed and under all road conditions.

The weight of the pistons was controlled to one-hundredth of an ounce. The pistons were partially machined before being heat-treated to remove internal casting stresses. This is the main reason that *Wills Sainte Claire* vehicles developed very few carbon deposits over many miles. Another reason is the Wills pressure lubrication system, a necessity for any smooth-running engine. The cooling system included a thermostatic device that regulated the flow and circulation of water.

The braking system was hydraulic. The *Wills Sainte Claire* was, along with the *Rickenbacker*, the first mass-produced auto with four-wheel brakes.

Known for developing a new version of the planetary transmission for Ford's *Model T*, in his own cars, Wills used a sliding type with center control. Like most parts, the gears and shafts were made of molybdenum steel. There were roller bearings at all points, except for the sliding gear shaft, where double ball bearings were used.

By 1922, the car was seemingly successful when it sold out all the 1921 models produced. However, fifteen hundred cars were the breakeven point, and the factory had only produced nine hundred. This was despite the fact that on June 5, 1922, eighty cars were assembled in a single day, a company record. Wills called for a doubling of production for the year to follow.

It was a surprise, therefore, when, in November 1922, the company went into "friendly receivership" due to a petition from the **Michigan Malleable Iron Company**. The **C.H. Wills & Company** was more than $8 million in debt.

The early 1920s was not a favorable time to build cars. After World War I, parts shortages caused some companies, like the **Regal Motor Company** and the **Hackett Motor Car Company**, to fail. Some firms, like the **Dodge Motor Car Company**, saw production reduced to just a third of what it had been. A postwar recession and labor shortage due to the war and the influenza epidemic added to the problems of the new auto company.

Another reason often cited for the company's first failure is Wills's perfectionism. He didn't want to let a car leave the door if he could somehow improve upon it. Whenever he thought of another improvement for the car, however small, he would stop the assembly line. Workers would wait while the entire operation was retooled to apply Wills's latest improvement.

Wills would say to his sales department, "Why should I let that car go out, when a brief delay will permit me to make it better?" Wills preferred building great cars to just filling orders. This has probably been exaggerated, but it's true that Wills had a passion for car building that he passed on to his workers and staff. A more probable reason for less-than-predicted sales was the shaky postwar economy. As it was, the company had many more orders than it could fill. (The car was that good!)

Due to the debt the company had built up, the **C.H. Wills & Company** Board of Directors thought it could never recover. All of the board members resigned, including John R. Lee.

10

RECEIVERSHIP AND REBIRTH

C.H. Wills wasn't ready to quit. His reputation and passion helped him to convince the Boston firm Kidder, Peabody & Company to finance the next year's models. Wills bought the company out of receivership, and a December 7, 1922 article in *Motor Age* magazine quoted Wills as saying that the company was solvent and that the court action was a way of rehabilitating the company and putting it on a strong financial basis. The company was reorganized as the **Wills Sainte Claire Motor Company**. Wills then started on the 1923 models with the new innovations and improvements he had devised.

During the bankruptcy debacle in 1922, Edsel Ford had convinced his father, Henry, to diversify **Ford Motor Company**. Sales of the *Model T* were down considerably. It was well known that the **Lincoln Motor Company** was in financial trouble, so the elder Ford decided to purchase the company. That it allowed Ford to deal a blow to Henry Leland, who had steered Ford's original company into becoming the **Cadillac Motor Company**, was an extra added bonus. After it was reported that Wills had lunch with Henry Ford, publicity surrounding the **Lincoln Motor Company** sale mentioned that the *Wills Sainte Claire* operation would also be purchased by Ford. Wills was quick to refute this.

In 1925, Wills was trying to cut down on manufacturing costs with the development of a taller but narrower six-cylinder engine that would be less expensive to produce than the V8s. There were also complaints about the V8 engine from mechanics, who preferred a less-complicated six-cylinder engine to work on.

Wills's V8 engine was extremely expensive, as well as hard to work on by the average "garage man," who didn't understand it as he did a four- or six-cylinder engine. Wills worked on a smaller engine that produced nearly the same horsepower that he felt would be worthy of his autos.

The *Wills Sainte Claire*s of 1926 included *Model C-68*, with eight cylinders, sixty-five horsepower and a 127-inch wheelbase available in all the different styles. The *Model A-6* was offered, with no changes made in the lineup from 1925. In 1926, an electric fuel pump was added.

It was not Wills's original intention that the high cost of the *Wills Sainte Claire* automobile put it into the already overcrowded "luxury auto" class. There were already more luxury cars being made than the market could handle, because there weren't enough high-earning people to buy them all. Wills was aiming for a middle market, like the one Buick covered. Instead, he ended up with a car that was more in the Cadillac price range.

The multitude of American luxury car brands included the "Three Ps": **Packard**, **Peerless** and **Pierce Arrow**. Other luxury brands included **Duesenberg**, **Cord**, **Auburn**, **Studebaker President**, **Cole**, **King**, **Standard**, **Kenworthy**, **Daniels**, **Kissell**, **Excalibur**, **LaSalle**, **Marmon**, **Cunningham** and **Stutz**, not to mention the *Chrysler Imperial*, **GM**'s *Cadillac* and the **Ford Motor Company**'s *Lincoln* brand.

In addition, there were European cars that appealed to America's tycoons, plutocrats and well-to-do class. These included **Rolls-Royce**, **Mercedes-Benz** and **Bugatti**, to name just a few. Wills had originally hoped to charge much less for the vehicles, but he couldn't bear to let them leave the factory unless they satisfied his perfectionism.

Further hampering sales was the fact that, in some circles, the *Wills Sainte Claire* was considered smaller and less elaborate than most luxury cars of the day, although the price tag was similar. The Wills cars did earn a great reputation for quality in the auto world, which was much more important to Wills.

There had been no major design changes for the 1922 models. For the 1923 models, Wills added a Brougham model—a five-passenger, closed car with a longer wheelbase. Also added was the 1923 *Gray Goose Traveler*, a sports car painted gray with red trim that sold for $2,775. The touring car, roadster, coupe, sedan, limo and town car continued to be offered. The *Model A-68* vehicles had a wheelbase of 121 inches, and its V8 engine could generate sixty-seven horsepower.

The *Model W-6* did not change models from 1922. It had a six-cylinder engine that generated sixty-six horsepower. The wheelbase was 127 inches.

In 1923, the same range of vehicles were available with six-cylinder engines. Known as *Model A-6*, it had a wheelbase of 121 inches, and the engine generated 66 horsepower.

The cars continued to be praised for their fine mechanics. All the cars Wills sold came with an owner's manual and maintenance instructions. These included a lubrication chart and instructions for servicing the car at intervals of two hundred, five hundred, one thousand, two thousand and five thousand miles. Production in 1923 amounted to 1,659 vehicles—not fabulous, but enough for the company to carry on for another year, with new models for 1924. Sales and production were up, and the sales force could now reach more than 80 percent of the United States, including many remote areas of the country.

The 1923 models were unveiled at the New York Automobile Show in the Grand Central Palace in mid-January and then went on to the Chicago Automobile Show in the Coliseum at the end of the month.

Wills never wanted to take his company public, preferring to retain full control, but in 1923, the inevitable happened. **Wills Sainte Claire** stock became publicly available.

A worker in the **Wills Sainte Claire** factory lubes the chassis of an early Wills auto.

Above: Auto workers in the Wills factory assembling the **Wills Sainte Claire**.

Left: An artisan working on one of the finer points of the **Wills Sainte Claire** engine.

A Wills employee machining an engine component of a *Wills Sainte Claire* auto. (The photos of the Wills laborers were originally shot as part of an advertising profile for the **Wills Sainte Claire Company**.)

For the 1924 models, Wills introduced balloon tires, hydraulic brakes and a long-stroke overhead camshaft. A six-cylinder engine replaced the expensive-to-build and hard-to-service V8 engine. Although the V8 could very quickly accelerate to seventy miles per hour and comfortably cruise at sixty miles per hour, it had a slight vibration problem. The six-cylinder model was very smooth but didn't handle as well.

The V8 engine still allowed the vehicle to get fourteen miles per gallon, which was exceptional for the time.

In 1924, *Wills Sainte Claire* cars came in ten different styles with two different models, A-68 and B-68. They were powered by a V8-cylinder, overhead cam engine that generated sixty-seven horsepower. A choice of 121- or 127-inch wheelbase was offered.

When Wills introduced four-wheel hydraulic brakes in 1924, the auto world had already seen front-wheel brakes on the 1923 *Rickenbacker* vehicles, produced by World War I aviator Eddie Rickenbacker. Fearing the competition, other companies broadcast the supposed danger of having front-wheel brakes stop the car. It was said it would most likely cause the vehicle to upset or even tip over. Rickenbacker backed off on the brakes the following year. This bad publicity did not deter Wills from introducing his four-wheel hydraulic brakes. He knew the superior aspects of the new brakes and didn't fear the scare tactics of the other companies.

There were *Models A-68* and *B-68* in 1924, and two new models were introduced, the *Imperial Sedan* and the *Gray Goose Special*. There was also a five-passenger Brougham model and the *Model A-68 V8 Rumble-Seat Roadster*, designed to be the showcase for the Wills V8 engine. The *B-68* was the larger model, with a 127-inch wheelbase.

The 1924 models featured a quieter engine, a result of a revised firing order, providing less vibration and improved lubrication. The horsepower was increased to sixty-five, and one of the car's features was a bracket on the door to enable holding a set of golf clubs. The total production for 1924 was 2,162 automobiles.

Between 1924 and 1925, it was decided that the car must be produced more inexpensively, even though sales and production had improved. Therefore, in 1925, mechanics were happy when Wills introduced the new inline six-cylinder engine (the W6), with an overhead camshaft but a detachable cylinder head. Customers were also happy with the new engine (although Wills continued to produce the superior V8). The name of the *Gray Goose Special* was changed to *Gray Goose Traveler*. A new model was the seven-passenger Phaeton.

C.H. Wills in pictured in his Marysville **Wills Sainte Claire** factory.

The 1925 models included the eight-cylinder, sixty-seven-horsepower *B-68*, available in the 121- or 127-inch wheelbase. The six-cylinder, sixty-six-horsepower *Model W-6* was available in only the 127-inch wheelbase. The *Models A-68* and *C-68* were available with an advance order. In 1925, the "Autopulse" electric fuel pump was added to cars with the W6 engine.

The Wills plant was not above customizing a vehicle, as long as the customer was paying for it. Employee Earl Minor recalled a "deluxe version" of the seven-seater limousine that was built for a maharajah. In fact, it was so deluxe that employees were not allowed to sit in it. One day, at lunchtime, Earl went to look at what was coming down the assembly line and spotted the maharajah's car. Unable to resist, he looked around and, seeing no one watching, proceeded to sit in the car. He immediately noticed the high thread count of the upholstery. He could feel the additional comfort in the seat cushions provided by the many sacks of goose down, specially imported directly from India.

A fight resulted when Earl fell asleep on the vehicle's comfortable seats and was caught by his foreman. However, in the end, the entire factory came through to admire and feel pride in the car they had all produced.

Still, the total production was down for the year—the total for 1925 was 1,829. The writing was beginning to appear on the wall when the *Gray Goose Bulletin* of November 1925 announced that the general sales department would be relocating from Marysville to 500 East Jefferson in Detroit, the location of the Wills Detroit dealership. It was bragged that one could go from the Interurban Railroad stop by the dealership straight to the Marysville factory to pick up one's *Wills Sainte Claire* automobile.

Wills would later expand the factory service schools for mechanic training and teach mechanics how to work on the new V8 engines. This would help the service departments immensely.

11

THE GREAT CONTINENTAL TREK

On July 14, 1925, a 1925 unaltered *Wills Sainte Claire Model W-6 Roadster* was used to set a new transcontinental speed record. Louis B. Miller, an automobile accessories dealer from San Francisco, drove from New York to San Francisco.

Miller, known as the "King of the Lincoln Highway," was no stranger to coast-to-coast trips. While still a child, he made three trips from San Francisco to New York on his bicycle. His first coast-to-coast auto trip didn't end well. The car fell apart, and he ended up mailing the only remaining parts—the horn and the steering wheel—back to the company.

The 3,423-mile trip in the *Wills Sainte Claire* was made by Miller with much greater success. He not only finished with the car in tip-top shape, but he also beat the previous record by seven hours and forty-five minutes. Miller knew that he had at last found the car with the power, durability and, most important to Miller, the comfort, to beat the intercontinental record.

Miller was past his prime, age fifty, when he set out to drive the *Wills Sainte Claire* to a record. Per his account, he drove the whole voyage himself, going without sleep for four days. A. Hansen, his assistant, had the job of navigating and keeping Miller from falling asleep. According to Hansen, Miller drove the whole way except for 750 miles, which Hansen said he drove. Regardless, the entire trip was completed in 102 hours and 45 minutes.

Miller continued to admire the car's performance. Arriving in Iowa, he fired off a telegram to Wills: "The farther the car goes the better it gets."

L.B. Miller had a crowd to greet him after he broke the transcontinental automobile record in his **Wills Sainte Claire** roadster.

They set off down the Lincoln Highway and, four days later, pulled into San Francisco, having achieved their goal of setting a new transcontinental record. Their record time was called "The Most Remarkable Thing a Motor Car Has Ever Done."

News articles and advertisements trumpeted that the two men had accomplished the trip in less time than an express train could achieve it. Miller said the marathon was completed on a diet of a bag of oranges, ice cream from a thermos and plenty of black coffee. As for the car, Miller said that it did not need a "single, solitary mechanical adjustment of any kind during the entire trip." He also lauded the car for not needing even one drop of water in the radiator the whole way. They were helped along the way. For instance, in Pittsburgh, the Pittsburgh Rotary helped escort them through town as quickly as possible. By the end of the trip, Hansen was pouring ice water down Miller's neck to keep him awake.

In March 1926, in the effort to deliver a part for a much-needed x-ray machine, Miller set a new record, going from Portland, Oregon, to San Francisco in forty hours and fifty-three minutes. This run was done in a 1926 *Wills Sainte Claire Six Gray Goose Roadster*.

When Miller returned with the record, he went to Wills's house in Marysville, where he was awarded a brand-new **Wills Sainte Claire** sedan.

On August 28, 1926, Miller repeated his transcontinental New York–San Francisco trek, with passenger and Portland mechanic J.E. Wieber. This time, Miller was in a *Wills Sainte Claire Stock T-6 Roadster*, setting a new record with the vastly improved time of eighty-three hours and twelve minutes. He said that the disparity between the two times was a result of the greatly improved roads. In recognition of his accomplishment, Wills gave Miller a brand-new *Wills Sainte Claire*.

12

THE LAST DAYS OF THE WILLS SAINTE CLAIRE COMPANY

Production for 1926 was 2,085 autos. It would turn out to be the last year of steady production. The *Gray Goose Traveler* became just the *Traveler*.

On September 24, 1926, the company was dissolved, although it wasn't until 1928 that the land occupied by the Wills factory was sold. This was a tough time for car companies, as indicated by a list of firms that went out of business around the same time: **Apperson**, **Briscoe**, **Case**, **Chalmers**, **Chandler** (sold to **Hupp**), **Cole**, **Davis**, **Dort**, **Gray**, **Mercer**, **Rickenbacker**, **Rollins** and **Winton**.

As 1927 dawned, production was too low for the company to ever show a profit. Consequently, no new models were introduced for the year. Purportedly, the **Wills Sainte Claire Company** continued making custom autos with the parts it still had on hand. However, no official 1927 Wills cars have ever been verified.

In his usual way, Wills handled the failure of his company stoically. He said to his son, "That was yesterday, and we can't make any money off that."

In the early 1930s, Wills sold the building to Walter Chrysler. The next day, a portion of the **Illinois Tool Company** building was leased to the **Buhl Aircraft Company**, a subsidiary of **Buhl Stamping Company**.

Buhl Stamping Company was formed in 1888 by Theodore Buhl in Detroit. He was the son of Christian Buhl (1812–1894), who was mayor of Detroit in 1860 and 1861 and cofounder of the Michigan Bank. Christian Buhl had made a fortune in the wholesale hardware business.

Buhl Aircraft Company wasted no time and moved into the factory the day after Wills left. It had close ties to Wills, since Buhl owned a building in Marysville that Wills used to store parts. This building was originally sought to serve as the Wills Sainte Claire Museum.

In the Marysville factory, **Buhl Aircraft Company** produced a series of enclosed aircraft that would hold from three to eight people. These were called "airsedans," or the "Pup." The firm also made open cockpit planes called "airsters" that could seat between three and eight people. Among these were the Buhl CA-1 Airster and the Buhl-Verville CA-3 Airster. It also produced an experimental autogyro plane called the Buhl A-1 Autogyro. The planes were tested at the Packard Proving Grounds at Van Dyke Avenue and 23 Mile Road in Utica, Michigan. This was the grounds where **Packard Motor Company** had tested its vehicles. **Buhl Aircraft** also had an airstrip next to the Marysville factory.

When the Great Depression arrived in 1929, causing the demand for planes to wane, Buhl switched to producing a small, single-seat aircraft called the Buhl AirSedan. In 1930 and 1931, it produced a smaller, single-seat vehicle called the Buhl Pup. **Buhl Aircraft** went out of business in 1933.

Buhl aircraft set many speed and endurance records. On August 15, 1929, the Buhl AirSedan *Spokane Sun-God* became the first aircraft to make a nonstop U.S. transcontinental round-trip flight.

Wills couldn't bring himself to retire just yet. He worked as a consultant for **Timken Roller Bearing Company**, and then, in 1928, he was hired by **Chris-Craft Boats** to help build an engine for the 1928 **Chris-Craft** twenty-six-foot Sport Hydro boat. It was built at the **Chris-Craft** factory in Algonac, Michigan, not far from the Wills factory in Marysville. The engine, with the customary narrow and tall Wills design, wouldn't fit into the usual engine casings, but once it was modified and put in the hydro-boat, it zoomed right by Gar Wood, the famed boating racer, who also lived in the Algonac area.

In 1929, Wills, along with some of his men, got involved with the building of the *Ruxton* automobile. He performed a small amount of help on the prototype and was on the board of directors of **New Era Motors**, the company organized to manufacture the car.

The *Ruxton* was prized in its day as one of the first cars to have a front-wheel drive. (The *Cord L-29* of the **Auburn Motor Company** of Auburn, Indiana, was probably the first.) However, the car had a checkered history that led to the ruination of four auto companies. This happened even though the Ruxton firm boasted many fine employees formerly employed

Mary and Harold Wills in the late 1930s.

at the **Wills Sainte Claire** factory, including machine specialist and tool designer Oscar C. Bornholdt; machine-tool expert Charles Morgana, who had been a Wills vice-president; sales manager William Purvis; metallurgist and Wills protégé Henry T. Chandler; and Wills himself.

When the *Ruxton* failed, Wills, although still financially independent, felt he was too young to retire. Even though he had lost $13 million on his *Wills Sainte Claire* investment, he still had plenty of money left. Yet, he still wanted to keep busy.

He contacted his friend George Holley, who still worked at **Ford Motor Company**, to see if he could come back. Holley contacted Henry Ford, who turned the decision over to his chief production manager and head of security, Charles E. Sorenson. This was the same Sorenson who had never liked Wills. Neither did Ford's friend Harry Bennet. The response was negative; Wills would not be welcomed back to the company he had helped start.

Wills also checked with the **Willys-Overland Company**. It owned the **Falcon Motor Car Company**, which produced the *Falcon-Knight*, a "parts-bin" car assembled from the parts of other Willys autos—the *Willys-Knight* and the *Whippet*. Wills made a bid to produce the car for the firm, but it didn't happen. The **Willys-Overland Company** replaced the car in 1928 with the *Willys-Knight 56 Standard Six*, which was similar to the *Falcon-Knight* automobile.

Wills started working for **Chrysler** as chief metallurgist and consultant in 1933. Prior to this position, he had been researching at Amola Steel. He continued to work on metallurgy for **Chrysler** for eight years until his death in 1940. At first, he was hired at a low salary and placed in an office with two others, but he soon earned his own office and private secretary.

Once Wills started working for the **Chrysler Motor Company**, he moved to 930 Lakeshore Drive in Grosse Pointe Farms. He continued his research on the construction of better auto bodies. When he developed new all-steel construction techniques for cars, he was awarded still more patents. He also invented a "sealed-beam" headlight and was involved in the development of "Oilite Bearings" for **Chrysler**.

Wills continued to develop, with the assistance of Fred E. McLeary and a team of metallurgists, the alloy known as Amola Steel, a lightweight but very durable material used by Chrysler in its *Chrysler Airflow*. The *Airflow* was a full-sized car produced by the firm from 1934 to 1937. Amola Steel was also used for razor blades. **Chrysler** bought a metal blend patent from Wills.

When he started at **Chrysler**, Wills, who never spent much time in his office in whatever job he had, would wander through the corridors of the company, checking on production and taking notes. His observations and suggestions saved Chrysler over $350,000 in production costs each year.

A story in *Motor Age* magazine related an incident when Wills was at **Boyer Machine Company**. His supervisor there had advised him, "Aim high and you'll never shoot low." Wills had taken the advice to heart and so was disheartened when he found his old supervisor down on his luck, sponging off his relatives. Wills asked the man what he would most like to be doing and was given the reply, "Running a chicken farm." Much to the former supervisor's dismay, Wills returned a few weeks later and handed him the deed to a chicken farm and a bank statement showing $5,000 in an account in the man's name to be used in the maintenance of the farm. Wills called it "deferred payment" for the advice. At the time of the 1921 article, the supervisor was successfully raising two thousand chickens on his farm.

Wills was a millionaire before the age of forty. When asked by a reporter what it was like to be a millionaire, he said that, as a young man, he'd heard a female friend call another man a genius for saving $10,000 in ten years. Wills met that mark. Then another of his friends said how wonderful it would be to have $100,000, a sum sure to produce an annual income of $6,000 a year. Again, Wills accomplished just that. The new goal became

$500,000, then $1,000,000. Once he had his first million, Wills sat down to consider what it meant. He concluded that he "was in a few more clubs, [his] personal expenses were more, [he] had a few more luxuries—and a few more relatives." But he was no happier and couldn't work any harder or find more enjoyment in what he did. Nor was his future any brighter. It was then that it dawned on him what a fortune really meant. He learned that it gave him "a greater opportunity to serve the community and make life happier for other people by making it possible for them to achieve happiness through their own efforts."

When Wills died of a diabetes-induced stroke on December 28, 1940 (in Henry Ford Hospital), he was still a wealthy man. Sadly, though, he was still relatively young, sixty-two. Wills was leaning on a stairwell while fixing a lamp when he fell and struck his head. His doctor, who knew he was diabetic, was out of town. The doctors at the hospital were treating him only for a concussion. Wills lapsed into a diabetic coma and died two days after.

Henry Ford made one of his rare public appearances when he attended Wills's funeral.

13

THE LEGACY OF
C. HAROLD WILLS

Many articles and accounts of C. Harold Wills since his death emphasized his role as an unsung pioneer of the automobile's early days. It has already been documented how Henry Ford did not give many other people credit for his industry successes. But the owners and fans of the *Wills Sainte Claire* automobiles researched and knew of Wills's accomplishments. They kept in touch to find and trade parts for their Wills autos, as most owners of "orphan" cars must do. An orphan car is one that is no longer being made. Besides the appreciation shown by old-timers, the beauty of Wills's auto creations continued to gain fans years after their original production.

In 1933, **Chrysler Motor Company** bought the former Wills factory and retooled it to be used once more for an auto company. In 2000, **Chrysler** demolished the building and constructed a new, twenty-two-thousand-square-foot parts facility. This structure now houses Chrysler's Mopar division.

In January 1959, in Kissimmee, Florida, Kenneth Caldwell formed the Wills Club in tribute to C. Harold Wills and to stay in communication with other *Wills Sainte Claire* auto owners. Caldwell and the members started a newsletter, the *Gray Goose News*, and with it contacted and communicated with owners of Wills autos all over the world.

The first copy of the newsletter contained Ken Caldwell's article "The Care and Operation of Wills Sainte Claire Motor Cars." Besides including members' writings about their *Wills Sainte Claires* and inquiries for parts, the newsletter contained advertisements for Ken Caldwell's original, self-manufactured *Wills Sainte Claire* products, including a strap to hold down the Wills Roadster top, a Flying Goose radiator cap ornament and authentic *Wills Sainte Claire* parts.

In 1976, the Wills Club organized the first National Meet in Marysville, Michigan. Flying in on his private jet from Reno, Nevada, was casino owner William "Bill" Harrah, the most famous car collector in the world. He owned thirteen *Wills Sainte Claires* and had eight of them shipped out for the festivities. He had written an issue of the *Gray Goose News* (at the time, each member was required to write an issue).

It was not difficult to entice each member to write an issue of the *Gray Goose News*. Everyone who owned a *Wills Sainte Claire* had a story to tell. Each Wills owner felt a certain affinity for the car that was years ahead of its time.

In 1977, a historical marker for the original Wills factory was proposed, and it was approved in 1983. The marker arrived in December 1983, and a large crowd attended the dedication on August 19, 1984. It was the first historical marker in Marysville.

The third National Meet was held in 1990 in Marysville and once more was a big success.

Bill McKeand of Port Huron passionately carried on with the Wills Club and newsletter until his untimely death in 1996 at the age of forty-seven. Jim Caldwell, son of Wills Club founder Ken, took over the newsletter but, due to work obligations, was unable to keep up with the correspondence. As the club declined, member Fred Cleaver requested that Terry Ernest take on the duties, which he did shortly before 1999.

The first order of business was updating the list of *Wills Sainte Claire* owners originally compiled by Bill McKeand. Carl Moss contacted members and updated the list as members sold their cars or passed away.

Gilmore Car Museum in Hickory Corners is the kind of museum you would expect to find in Michigan, the home of many motor marques and of the Motor City itself. Located on ninety acres, the museum comprises twelve buildings full of old cars, not to mention a nostalgic restaurant and gas station. In 1999, Wills president Terry Ernest met future Wills Sainte Claire Museum benefactor Richard Donahey of Belleville, Michigan, who happened to own a building in Terry's hometown of Marysville, Michigan.

Soon, a correspondence began with e-mail during that mode of communication's early days. An e-mail Terry Ernest wrote but hadn't intended to send suggested that Mr. Donahey donate his building to the

Wills Club. This was since it was on Wills Street. The e-mail somehow got sent, and Ernest received a reply: "I'll consider it!"

Lawyers went back and forth, and the building was eventually donated by Donahey to the Wills Club to "create a place where the technology and history of C. Harold Wills could be shared and used for educational purposes." The club filed paperwork to become a nonprofit organization, and the club transitioned into a museum.

In 2002, the long-planned museum in honor of C. Harold Wills and the *Wills Sainte Claire* automobile was opened, in the building donated by Richard and Patricia Donahey. The building, located not far from the former Wills plant, was erected by Dow Chemical in 1943, during World War II. It was originally constructed for wartime testing of the explosive qualities of magnesium. It has some unique features. For instance, in case the building explodes (as it might with experimental munitions), the roof will blow off without serious damage to the basic structure, which is concrete with wooden trusses and roof.

In forming the museum's collections, Bill McKeand managed to obtain the Florida group's collection, including the newsletter archive of the Wills Club. McKeand was so instrumental in obtaining documents and other

Wills Sainte Claire Museum volunteers attending the local AACA Blue Water Region car show in Marysville, Michigan, in June 2017.

information that the research room of the Wills Museum was named the "Wm. McKeand Research Room" in his honor.

One of the notable *Wills Sainte Claire* collectors was Tom Lieb of Torrance, California. His collection of *Wills Sainte Claire* cars included the 1921 A-68 Touring Car, a 1923 roadster model, an unrestored 1921 four-door sedan, a 1923 seven-passenger sedan and two 1926 roadsters. Like museum founder Terry Ernest and curator Carl Moss, Lieb had written about the *Wills Sainte Claire* in auto magazines. In early 2008, he donated two 1926 *Wills Sainte Claires* to the Wills Sainte Claire Auto Museum in Marysville.

Other acquisitions of the museum include a drill press used in the original Wills plant and a 1920s Fry gas pump. The drill press was so heavy, it required two tow trucks to move it from its Marysville bus garage location to the Wills Museum.

In the late 1960s, another group of antique car enthusiasts began communicating with one another and, by 1970, were having regular meetings. They met on the second Thursday of the month at the St. Clair County Library, located in Port Huron, and called themselves the Antique Auto Enthusiasts. The band of auto enthusiasts continued to meet over the years and became a close-knit group. Some of the original classic cars owned by this group included a 1931 *Model A* and a 1949 *Packard*. This group disbanded, and many of the members joined the local chapter of the Antique Automobile Club of America (AACA), Blue Water Region, which is also associated with the Wills Museum.

14

THE WILLS SAINTE CLAIRE MUSEUM

The final step to preserving the legacy of C. Harold Wills was the Wills Sainte Claire Museum. The newsletter continued to keep the Wills car owners in touch. The current incarnation of the newsletter, with Terry Ernest as editor, has won numerous awards, including the Golden Quill Award for numerous consecutive publications over the years. The Wills Sainte Claire Museum has won six "NAAMY" awards, given by the National Association of Automobile Museums (NAAM).

The Donahey Foundation, put together by Richard and Patricia Donahey, initially benefited the museum with its building, paid utilities and many other amenities. Renovations to the building have been mostly executed by the members of the museum themselves.

The museum's first board of directors, including Terry Ernest (director), Fred Cleaver (treasurer), Gary Wurmlinger (vice-president) and Carl Moss (secretary and curator) was instrumental in getting the museum started. Some members have been with the museum since the start.

Members of the Wills family have also become involved with the museum. One of Wills's granddaughters, Sally Wills Achatz, sits on the board of directors for the Wills Museum. Mary Ann Nester (whose husband, Robert, was Wills's grandson), contributed the pictures of C. Harold's parents and children when they were young.

Due to Wills and his autos, the town of Marysville continues to grow. When Wills moved to Marysville, the population quickly went from less than two hundred to more than three thousand people. Many of the industries attracted to this town by Wills remain, and Wills's legacy goes on as the patron of Marysville. However, as one of the museum's founders, Carl Moss, said, "One of the reasons we wanted to open the museum is because 80 percent of the residents of Marysville had never heard of C. Harold Wills or the Wills Sainte Claire autos."

In June 2016, Wills Museum president Terry Ernest drove a *Wills Sainte Claire* auto to its one-time owner, Bill Mason, for his 100th birthday, proving that *Wills Sainte Claire* owners are often as resilient as the car.

Of the 12,107 *Wills Sainte Claire* autos that were built, only about 80 remain—and the Wills Museum has 17 of the remaining cars on display. It's the largest collection of Wills cars in the world. The museum also houses a large archive, including many of the original Wills documents and the collection of the Wills Club.

The museum has established an annual award, the Spirit of C.H. Wills Award. Museum president and *Gray Goose News* newsletter editor Terry Ernest explained: "C. Harold Wills was a man of amazing vision and foresight. Since his early days of working with Henry Ford, he envisioned an automobile of high quality built by a contented workforce who lived in modern homes in a true community. The Spirit of C.H. Wills award is given by the Museums' Board of Directors in tribute to this spirit."

The board members are not eligible to receive the award.

The Spirit of C.H. Wills Award winners are as follows:

2002	Steve Rossi and John Porter
2003	Fred Cleaver and Bruce Frumveller
2004	Marlene Porter, Harold Krul and Karl Krouch Sr.
2005	Mike Lauth, Rosemary Cleaver and Bill Carlisle
2006	Don Herber and Rita Ernest
2007	Gregg Cleaver and Paul Pawlosky
2008	Tom Lieb and Stan Mitchell
2009	Jerry Saunders and Rudy Vernon
2010	Gary Minnie and Jerry Taylor
2011	Debbie Wurmlinger and Ed Hausgen
2012	Ed Hausgen
2013	Ray Burgess
2014	Gary Wurmlinger
2015	Kay Carlisle
2016	Scott Shepley

Chronicling the award named for a generous man who wanted to make life better for the workingman while being conscientious enough to want to make every single automobile he sold the best that it could be, is a good place to conclude Wills's story.

OR, WHEN LEGEND BECOMES FACT

Writing about C. Harold Wills, a true unsung auto pioneer, has mostly involved chasing down old newspaper articles and references in obscure books to get as close to the truth as possible. Especially in an era when everyone who ever personally knew your subject is gone, it's best to try to obtain accounts as close to the actual happenings as possible. Therefore, newspaper accounts, usually written soon after an occurrence, are likely to be more accurate than people's memories of memories of an occurrence. The closer an account of an incident is to the time that it really happened, the more accurate it will probably be. Memories tend to fade over time.

One usually wants to find two sources to be sure of a fact. In the case of Wills, there has been a great deal of admiration for him and his accomplishments among the coterie of people who own Wills cars. So the Wills Club, and later the Wills Sainte Claire Museum, have faithfully archived the pertinent information about Wills. There have been few conflicts in facts.

This is good news, since, when facts conflict with a good story, the good story becomes "the legend," and people want to believe the legend. In lives that are commonly bland and mundane, the fantastic, with a tinge of magic, gives one more pleasure than a stale old history fact. It's been noted that if you ask three different people from three different angles to give their account of a traffic accident, you will get three distinct and sometimes different stories, each time told with a little more embellishment.

This is perhaps why reporters and authors, to get a "good" story, will print the legend—even when they know the truth. When this happens enough times, you will be able to find the obligatory "two references" for a topic, and the legend becomes "fact." I don't think that has happened here—for one reason, the museum has archived many items that qualify as prime sources and that date to Wills's lifetime, including personal diaries. In addition, the oral histories recorded have been timely, revealed not long after the history has been made.

There have been a few quandaries matching facts to a Wills timeline, but one of the only items that seems to be more legend than fact is the mystery of the 1927 *Wills Sainte Claire*. *The Standard Catalog of Automobiles*, usually a valuable resource, states that the factory advertised that it would custom-make a Wills with the parts that were left if it was pre-ordered. The catalog said: "For 1927 it was announced that a car (with a V-8 engine) could be produced by special order. The *Gray Goose Traveler* was back with its full name, as well as an *Enclosed Drive Limo* but the end was near, as production, probably achieved with parts left over, totaled less than 330 units." This portion, while interesting, is doubtful.

There have also been a few sources that purport to show a 1927 *Wills Sainte Claire*, as well as a few that state that the *Wills Sainte Claire* was manufactured from 1921 to 1927. The museum has yet to verify an actual 1927 Wills auto.

This story might have its origins in Dallas Winslow's 1927 purchase of extra parts from the Wills factory. He also purchased Auburn, Cord and Duesenberg parts and would sell them to owners of these cars. Beyond that, it appears the 1927 *Wills Sainte Claire* might fall in the "legend" category.

Having the benefit of perspective, being able to view Wills from an age long after he has been gone, added to the pleasure of writing about Wills and having all the resources available from the archives of the Wills Museum.

BIBLIOGRAPHY

Automobile Topics: The Trade Authority. "As a Boomerang, It Comes Back." 63 (October 29, 1921): 892.

Baldwin, Nick, G.N. Georgano, Brian Laban, and Michael Sedgwick. *The World Guide to Automobile Manufacturers.* New York: Facts on File, 1987.

Barber, H.L. *Story of the Automobile: Its History and Development from 1760 to 1917.* Chicago: J.J. Munson & Company, 1917.

Benson Ford Archives. Dearborn, Michigan.

Bryan, Ford R. *Clara: Mrs. Henry Ford.* Detroit, MI: Wayne State University Press, 2001.

———. *Henry's Lieutenants.* Detroit, MI: Wayne State University Press, 1993.

Caldwell, Ken. *Gray Goose News.* Kissimmee, FL: Self-published, 1959–73.

Clarke, Edward L. "Wills Sainte Claire Motor Cars." *Antique Automobiles* 38, no. 2 (March–April 1974): 6–19.

Crabb, Richard. *Birth of a Giant.* Philadelphia, PA: Chilton Book Company, 1969.

Dahlinger, John Cole. *The Secret Life of Henry Ford.* Indianapolis, IN: Bobbs-Merrill Company, 1978.

DePalma Manufacturing Company. Corporate notes (1916–21).

Duricy, Dave. "Wheels for the Soul." *Cars & Parts* 53, no. 5 (May 2010): 40–45.

Epstein, Ralph C. *The Automobile Industry: Its Economic and Commercial Development.* Chicago: A.W. Shaw Company, 1928.

Ernest, Terry, ed. *Gray Goose News*. Marysville, MI: Wills Sainte Claire Museum, 2005–17.

Fitzgerald, Warren. "Wills Sainte Claire." *Car Life* (February 1967): 45–50.

Forbes, Bertie Charles and Orline, Dorman Foster. *Automotive Giants of America: Men Who Made Our Motor History*. Ancarano, Italy: Edizioni Savine, 1927.

Ford, Henry, and Samuel Crowther. *My Life and Times: Autobiography of Henry Ford*. Garden City, NY: Doubleday, Page & Company, 1922.

Georgano, G.N. *The Complete Encyclopedia of Motorcars: 1885 to the Present*. New York: E.P. Dutton and Company, 1973.

Glancy, Jonathan. *The Car: A History of the Automobile*. London, UK: Carlton Publishing Group, 2008.

Glasscock, C.B. *Motor History of America or The Gasoline Age*. Los Angeles: Floyd Clymer Publications, 1937.

Goldstone, Lawrence. *Drive! George Selden and the Race to Invent the Auto Age*. New York: Ballantine Books, 2016.

Graves, Ralph Henry. *The Triumph of an Idea: The Story of Henry Ford*. Garden City, NY: Doubleday, Doran & Company, 1934.

Gray Goose Bulletin (1922–25). Various authors. Marysville, MI: House organ.

Gray Goose (1972–present). Various authors and editors. Marysville, MI: Official newsletter of the Wills Club and the Wills Sainte Claire Museum.

Henry, M.D. "Childe Harold Wills: A Career in Cars." *Automobile Quarterly* (Fall 1966): 136–45.

Kimes, Beverly Rae. *The Cars That Henry Ford Built: A Commemorative Tribute to America's Most Remembered Automobiles*. Iola, WI: Krause Publications, 2004.

———. *Pioneers, Engineers, and Scoundrels: The Dawn of the Automobile in America*. Warrendale, PA: SAE International, 2005.

Kimes, Beverly Rae, and Henry Austin Clark Jr. *Standard Catalog of American Cars*. 1985. Revised edition, Iola, WS: Krause Publications, 1996.

Koch, Jeff. "Tom Lieb—Wills Sainte Claire Expert." *Hemmings Classic Car* 1, issue 8 (May 2005): 82–84.

Kowalke, Ron. *Standard Catalog of Independents: The Struggle to Survive Among Giants*. Iola, WI: Krause Publications, 1999.

Leonard, Jonathan Norton. *The Tragedy of Henry Ford*. New York: G.P. Putnam & Sons, 1932.

Ludvigsen, Karl, and David Burgess Wise. *The Encyclopedia of the American Automobile*. New York: Exeter Books, 1982.

MacManus, Theodore F. *Men, Money, and Motors*. New York: Harper & Brothers, 1929.

Marquis, Samuel S. *Henry Ford: An Interpretation.* Detroit, MI: Wayne State University Press, 2007.

May, George S. *A Most Unique Machine: The Michigan Origins of the American Automobile Industry.* Grand Rapids, MI: William B. Eerdmans Publishing Company, 1975.

May, George S., ed. *The Automobile Industry, 1920–1980.* Vols.1 & 2. New York: Facts on File, 1980–88.

McConnell, Curt. *Great Cars of the Great Plains.* Lincoln: University of Nebraska Press, 1995.

Miller, G. Wayne. *Car Crazy: The Battle for Supremacy between Ford and Olds and the Dawn of the Automobile Age.* New York: Public Affairs, 2015.

Nevins, Allan. *Ford: The Times, the Man, the Company.* New York: Charles Scribner's Sons, 1954.

Nevins, Allan, and Frank Ernest Hill. *Ford: Expansion and Challenge, 1915–33.* New York: Charles Scribner's Sons, 1957.

Rae, John Bell. *American Automobile Manufacturers: The First Forty Years.* Philadelphia, PA: Chilton Publishing Company, 1959.

Richardson, Jim. "American Beauty: Exploring the Detailed Beauty of a 1921 Wills Sainte Claire." *Special Interest Autos* no. 198 (November/December 2003): 24–29.

Snow, Richard. *I Invented the Modern Age: The Rise of Henry Ford.* New York: Scribner, 2013.

Stevens, Bob. "New Museum Honors the Wills Sainte Claire." *Cars & Parts* 47, no. 9 (September 2004): 34–37.

Sullivan, Frank. *The Ultimate History of American Cars: The Fascinating Story of America's Favorite Cars.* Bath, UK: Paragon Publishing, 2006.

Sward, Keith. *The Legend of Henry Ford.* New York: Rinehart & Company, 1948.

Szudarek, Robert G. *How Detroit Became the Automotive Capital.* Detroit, MI: Typocraft Company, 1996.

Wills Motor Company. Corporate notes. 1928.

"Wills Sainte Claire Motor Cars." *Cars & Parts* 11, no. 2 (November 1967): 19–29.

Wills Sainte Claire Museum Archives. Marysville, Michigan.

Woodward, Jack (August–October 1977). *Childe Harold Wills.* Bennington, VT: Special Interest Autos, 30-33.

INDEX

ABOUT THE AUTHORS

Alan Naldrett is an author from Chesterfield, Michigan. He has written books for Arcadia Publishing's Images of America series on Chesterfield and coauthored books on New Baltimore and Fraser, as well as contributing to *Ira Township*. By himself, he has written *Forgotten Tales of Lower Michigan*, *Lost Tales of Eastern Michigan* and *Lost Car Companies of Detroit*. He is an archivist and has recently been helping to organize archives and create finding aids for various entities, including townships, colleges, schools, churches and museums.

In his early days at Michigan State University, he started one of the first used-record shops in the nation. Moving to California after graduation, he ran an insurance agency and played in a band. Upon his return to Michigan, he opened a comic book store while he worked on master's degrees in library & information & archival sciences. He is now a retired research librarian.

Lynn Lyon Naldrett was an author on *Ira Township* in the Images of America series and has assisted Alan on his other books. She has done missionary work in India, has a master's degree in Usui Reiki and is a former board member and coordinator for MCREST. She organized fundraisers for charitable organizations, including churches and schools. A member of the Chesterfield and New Baltimore Historical Societies, she conducts and assists in many historical presentations.

Alan and Lynn could not believe that there had never been a biography written about C. Harold Wills and the Wills Sainte Claire auto. Hopefully, this is now sufficiently rectified!